Understanding the Indian Economy from the Post-Reforms of 1991, Volume I

Understanding the Indian Economy from the Post-Reforms of 1991, Volume I

History, Evolution, and Growth

Shrawan Kumar Singh

BEP BUSINESS EXPERT PRESS

Understanding the Indian Economy from the Post-Reforms of 1991, Volume I: History, Evolution, and Growth

First published in 2020 by
Business Expert Press, LLC
222 East 46th Street, New York, NY 10017
www.businessexpertpress.com

ISBN-13: 978-1-95152-740-2 (paperback)
ISBN-13: 978-1-95152-741-9 (e-book)

Business Expert Press Economics and Public Policy Collection

Collection ISSN: 2163-761x (print)
Collection ISSN: 2163-7628 (electronic)

Cover and interior design by S4Carlisle Publishing Services Private Ltd., Chennai, India

First edition: 2020

10 9 8 7 6 5 4 3 2 1

Printed in the United States of America.

Abstract

This is the first in a series of eight such volumes. An understanding of the Indian economy will be of help in more than one way. Since almost every problem has an economic angle, knowledge about the performance of various sectors of the Indian economy provides an opportunity to see things in a wider perspective. The present volume provides a snapshot of and analyzes the history, evolution, and growth of the Indian economy through several periods along with their positive and negative aspects. The periods covered are Paleolithic period to 1200 CE, the early Muslim period and the Mughal Empire (1200 to 1760), the British regime (1761 to 1947), and post-independence India (1947 to 1990). Points of analysis include policy framework—state and market; NITI Aayog—a think tank; the Indian polity—fiscal federalism; democracy and development; the economic policy regime prior to 1991; economic reforms; the present state of the economy and the task ahead; and Indian economic thought/thinkers.

The series that follow will cover agriculture, manufacturing, and service sectors of the economy in detail. In terms of employed population, India is largely an agrarian country. Nearly 50 percent of the Indian population depends on agriculture and allied activities for livelihood. But if contribution to the gross domestic product (GDP) is taken as the parameter, India is predominantly a service economy with the service sector having nearly 60 percent share of the total GDP. India, however, lags behind developed countries in the manufacturing sector. The Make in India initiative was taken in 2014 by the present government is a big step in this direction, toward making India an investment hub for manufacturing. The focus of the Make in India program is on job creation and skill enhancement in 25 sectors.

There are issues with agriculture, industry, services, and employment generation. The concerns related to macroeconomic stability in 2014 persist as fiscal deficit and current account deficit were higher than expected. The way forward for the economy in the coming years is for the government to stave off any nascent threats to macroeconomic stability, notably from persistently high oil prices and sharp, disruptive corrections to elevated asset prices. The penultimate chapter of this volume takes a look at the future direction and task ahead of the economy. There is plenty to discuss.

Keywords

Indian economy; post-reform; current account deficit; employment; fiscal federalism; fiscal deficit; inflation; macroeconomic stability

Contents

Preface

The Indian economy was, historically, one of the major economies of the world. India is a developing economy and is slowly but, as per World Bank indicators, steadily moving toward rapid economic activity and higher levels of income. It will be interesting to see how this is structured across the primary, secondary, and tertiary sectors. India's present economic fundamentals are associated with the problems of economic growth. A subject as vast as the postreform Indian economy rightly deserves a whole series of books. The series consists of eight volumes, numbered I through VIII. The aspects of the Indian economy covered in the series are History, Evolution, and Growth; Anatomy of the Indian Economy; Agrarian; Industrial; Financial Sector; Fiscal and Monetary Policy; External Sector Reforms; and Contemporary Issues in the Indian Economy. There are several important subtopics, such as natural resources and manpower, that present the readers with a good knowledge of how the Indian economy has evolved over the years.

Although India's economic growth has been impressive, it has been accompanied by a slow decline in poverty and unemployment, widening regional disparities, and vulnerability to balance-of-payments problems. India's growth has been unbalanced, both across the states and between the urban and rural areas. The service sector is the largest sector in the country at a low level of development. India's propoor growth strategy leads to long-term macroeconomic challenges. Corruption is associated with a lower level of economic growth.

Despite these problems, the Indian economy has registered impressive growth after the 1991 reforms. The demographics of a young population offer a distinct growth advantage. Service sector productivity has also increased after economic reforms. Sustaining growth seems to be feasible. Foreign trade is expected to serve as an engine of growth in future. India's share of the world's merchandise exports has been increasing.

Today, India is one of the most exciting emerging economies of the world. India's economy has been described as "huge, complex, and growing." It is said that the only way to describe the future is to shape it. As Gordon Gibbons had commented, "The winds and the tides always favour the ablest navigators." The past, present, and future of India represent the story of how the slow-growing economy in the first 40 years of independence became in the second phase, in the 1990s reforms, the 12th largest economy in the world. However, if the past is any guide to the future, political leadership of successive governments has broadly adhered to the ongoing reform program. India may have moved with caution but never backward. It cannot afford to "limit the realization of a better tomorrow to be deterred by doubts of today but must move forward with strong and active faith." India offers new and exciting investment and trade opportunities.

Acknowledgments

I am what I am because the elders of my generation exhorted, pampered, and showered their affection upon me with a generosity the current generation cannot even dream of. My indebtedness to all of them is immense and irredeemable. Although they were ever busy, they provide ample evidence to support the adage "Busy persons have time for everyone and for all matters." In writing a book, one draws upon the contributions of so many scholars. All efforts have been made to acknowledge the contributions of the authors the book has drawn upon, with detailed textual references given in the endnotes and the bibliography. I gratefully acknowledge the debt I owe to all such authors whose theories and views have provided me with ample wisdom and enlightenment. None of them are, however, responsible for the views that are expressed in the book and the errors that it might contain. I alone am responsible for errors and omissions, if any.

A special word of appreciation is due to my old friend D.P.S. Verma (retired professor of commerce, Delhi School of Economics, University of Delhi), who helped me in improving the presentation of my work and bringing it to its present format. Several friends, colleagues, and students had prompted me from time to time to write on the Indian economy. Several others have helped me in the actual writing of it. Foremost among them have been Dr. G.K. Arora (principal, Dr. Bhim Rao Ambedkar College, University of Delhi); Dr. Rabi Narayan Kar (principal, Shyam Lal College, University of Delhi); Dr. Sunil Ashra (professor of economics, Management Development Institute [MDI], Gurugram), Dr. S.S. Khanka (professor of management, Delhi Technological University, Delhi); Dr. Hukam Chand Jain (retired associate professor, Hansraj College, University of Delhi), Mr. Dhritman Gupta, Ph.D. Scholar at Indian Statistical Institute (ISI), Delhi chapter, Ms. Prachi Singh (consultant, NITI Aayog, Delhi), and Dr. Asmi Raza (associate professor, Zakir Husain College, University of Delhi) for their support.

The writing of any book causes a certain amount of domestic up-heaval. My family rode out the occasional pockets of turbulence with admirable fortitude. As always, my younger brother Mr. Prithwi Raj Singh of Satyawati College, University of Delhi provided his unstinted cooperation and support. In the development of this book, right from the very beginning, Mr. Manish Kumar Sharma has been a great source of strength in providing all the necessary secretarial assistance, and I express my special thanks to him. There is always scope for improvement, and I welcome comments, corrections, and suggestions from readers, which will be gratefully acknowledged and incorporated in the next edition. I eagerly look forward to receiving feedback at sksingheco71@gmail.com, for which I would be deeply grateful.

Shrawan Kumar Singh,
New Delhi (India)
September 30, 2019

CHAPTER 1

The Economic History of India from the Paleolithic Period to 1200 CE

Taking into account the importance of understanding the Indian economy, knowledge of its history is essential. This chapter attempts to discuss the history of the Indian economy in ancient times. India is one of the oldest civilizations in the world, and its economic history is at least 5,000 years old, dating back to the Indus Valley Civilization (DeFrain and Asay 2012). Ancient India was a rich country until foreigners plundered it for several hundred years. But it has a history of a great economy due to its trade relations with foreign countries ranging from those in the Far East to Western Europe and Africa.[1]

The earliest periods of Indian history are known only through reconstructions from archaeological evidence. Since the late 20th century, much new data has emerged, allowing a far fuller reconstruction than was formerly possible. Because of availability of this new data it is easier to frame the analysis into the following five major periods (Encyclopedia Britannica):

I. The early prehistoric period (before the 8th millennium BCE)
II. The period of the prehistoric agriculturalists and pastoralists (approximately the 8th to the mid-4th millennium BCE)
III. The Early Indus, or Early Harappan, Period (so named for the excavated city of Harappa in Eastern Pakistan), witnessing the emergence of the first cities in the Indus River system (c. 3500 to 2600 BCE)

IV. The Indus, or Harappan, Civilization (c. 2600 to 2000 BCE, or perhaps ending as late as 1750 BCE)

V. The Posturban Period, which follows the Indus Civilization and precedes the rise of cities in Northern India during the second quarter of the 1st millennium BCE (c. 1750 to 750 BCE)

The economy of a society is one of the most important factors in determining its progress. The Indus Valley people had developed a prosperous civilization on the basis of a thriving agricultural economy. It is interesting to note that the economic history of India begins with the Indus Valley Civilization (3300 to 1300 BCE), whose economy appears to have depended significantly on trade, most notably Indus–Mesopotamia trade relations. The Vedic Period, or Vedic Age (1500 to 500 BCE), is the period in the history of the Northern Indian subcontinent between the end of the urban Indus Valley Civilization and a second urbanization that began in the central Indo-Gangetic Plain (c. 600 BCE). During 1750–500 BCE Indo-Aryans settled into northern India, bringing with them specific religious traditions. Vedic society was patriarchal and patrilineal. The period saw countable units of precious metal being used for exchange.

The people were rural and agricultural. They domesticated animals like the cow, sheep, goat, ass, ox, and dog. People's wealth was known in terms of cattle rearing. Domestication of animals was a useful profession. People domesticated animals and birds for the purpose of milk, meat, and pleasure. Rig Vedic Indians (1500 to 500 BCE) also resorted to hunting for a livelihood. Mining was another important occupation, although the Aryans had not discovered iron during the Rig Vedic period. They had trade relations between themselves in the expanded lands formed by their migrations very early in their history. They produced wheat, barley, millet and a variety of fruits. The carpenter, the weaver, the potter, the goldsmith, the jeweler, the physician, and the house builder represented some other professions of this society. In the Later Vedic Period (1000 to 600 BCE), the economic life of the Aryans was well advanced and prosperous. The growth of cities was the best proof of this. Agriculture was still their main occupation, though. Cattle rearing was another important occupation. People were organized into guilds and had more extensive knowledge of different kinds of metals. Besides gold and copper, they also used silver and iron.

Then came the period of various empires in India, including the Gupta and the Mauryan Empires (325 to 185 BCE). India during the Mauryan period inevitably brings reference to the great king Ashoka. The Mauryan dynasty existed between the 4th and 3rd centuries BCE and unified the subcontinent for the first time and also contributed to the spread of Buddhism.

The Mauryan Empire brought large areas of land under cultivation. Land revenue was recognized as an important source of income. Assessment of land also took place at regular intervals. One-fourth of the national income was spent on public works and the salaries of the large staff. Public works included road construction, irrigation, rest house construction, and army maintenance. Iron was widely used. During excavations different types of iron tools like socketed axes, sickles, and possibly plowshares have been found. These tools must have made the task of clearing the thick forests of the Eastern Ganges plains easy. Additionally, these tools facilitated the efficiency of agriculture. Numerous small heaps of iron slogs have been found scattered all over the iron belt of South Bihar (Encyclopedia Britannica). Mauryan India had numerous private commercial entities. These existed purely for private commerce and developed before the Mauryan Empire itself.

The Gupta Empire existed from the mid-to-late 3rd century to 543 CE. It covered much of the Indian subcontinent. This period is considered the Golden Age of India by some historians. The most notable rulers of this dynasty were Chandragupta I, Samudragupta, and Chandragupta II (or Vikramaditya). The 5th century Sanskrit poet Kalidasa credits the Guptas with having conquered about 21 kingdoms, both in and outside India. Education played an important role in the Gupta Period. During the Gupta, period agriculture formed a significant part of the empire's economy. However, the trade and commerce activities of the Gupta Empire grew steadily. The merchant and other traders were organized into guilds. These guilds were given concessions in the taxes that were liable to be paid to the government.[2] During this era, primary education was obtained by the people. To obtain formal and higher education, people had to stay in *Brahmanical Agraharas*[3] or Buddhist monasteries.[4]

Trends in early Indian society: A considerable change is noticeable during this period in the role of institutions. Clan-based societies had assemblies, whose political role changed with the transformation of tribe into state and with oligarchic and monarchical governments. Centralized imperialism, which was attempted under the Mauryan Empire (325 to 185 BCE), gave way gradually to a decentralized administration and to what has been called a "feudalistic pattern" in the post-Gupta Period, that is, from the 7th century CE. Although the village as an administrative and social unit remained constant, its relationship with the mainstream of history varied. The pendulum of politics swung from large to small kingdoms, with the former attempting to establish empires—the sole successful attempt being that of the Mauryan dynasty. Thus, true centralization was rare, because local forces often determined historical events. These small kingdoms also often boasted the most elaborate and impressive monuments.

The major economic patterns related to land and to commerce. The transition from tribal to peasant society was a continuing process, with the gradual clearing of wasteland and the expansion of the village economy based on plow agriculture. Recognition of the importance of land revenue coincided with the emergence of the imperial system in the 4th century BCE, and from this period onward, although the imperial structure did not last long, land revenue became central to the administration and the income of the state. Frequent mentions of individual ownership, references to crown lands, numerous land grants to religious and secular grantees in the post-Gupta Period, and detailed discussions in legal sources of the rights of purchase, bequest, and sale of land all clearly indicate that private ownership of land existed. Much emphasis has been laid on the state control of the irrigation system; yet, a systematic study of irrigation in India reveals that it was generally privately controlled and serviced small areas of land. When the state built canals, they were mainly in the areas affected by both the winter and summer monsoons. Here, village assemblies played a dominant part in revenue and general administration, as in the Chola Kingdom of Southern India.

The urban economy was crucial to the rise of civilization in the Indus Valley (c. 2600 to 2000 BCE). Later, the 1st millennium BCE saw an urban civilization in the Ganges (Ganga) Valley and still later in coastal South

India. The emergence of towns was based on administrative needs, the requirements of trade, and pilgrimage centers. In the 1st millennium CE, when commerce expanded to include trade with Western Asia, the Eastern Mediterranean, and Central and Southeast Asia, revenue from trade contributed substantially to the economies of the participating kingdoms.

"Gold coins were issued for the first time by the Kushan dynasty (95 to 127 CE), and in large quantities by the Guptas. Both kingdoms were active in foreign trade. Gold was imported from Central Asia and the Roman Republic and Empire and later perhaps from Eastern Africa because, in spite of India's recurring association with gold, its sources were limited. Expanding trade encouraged the opening up of new routes, and this, coupled with the expanding village economy, led to a marked increase of knowledge about the subcontinent during the post-Mauryan period. With increasing trade, guilds became more powerful in the towns. Members of the guilds participated in the administration, were associated with politics, and controlled the development of trade through merchant embassies sent to places as far afield as Rome and China. Not least, guilds and merchant associations held envied and respectable positions as donors of religious institutions" (Encyclopedia Britannica).

Classical economic thoughts of India are based on the ideas of the Vedas, the Upanishads, the Epics, and so on. During the reign of Chandragupta, that is, in 300 BCE, Kautilya wrote a valuable book on economics titled *Arthashastra* (Kautilya (also known as Chanakya) was an Indian statesman and philosopher, chief advisor and Prime Minister of Emperor Chandragupta). The *Arthashastra* has continued to inspire nationalist economic historiography. Indian philosophers during ancient times stressed greatly on the equal distribution of produced commodities among the masses.

Sharma (2011) has pointed out as many as seven stages of the ancient Indian economy: (i) Harappan, (ii) Rg Vedic, (iii) Later Vedic, (iv) the period of c. 500 to 322 BC, (v) Mauryan, (vi) post-Mauryan (200 BC to 200 AD) and (vii) Gupta. He also touched upon the various modes of production, North Indian economic life during the Gupta Period, eight economic aspects of the caste system, the early medieval land grants, the peasant protest in early medieval India, usury in early medieval times, different aspects of urbanism along with urban growth and decline in early historic India.

Sharma (2011) dealt with the origins of Indian feudalism (300 to 750 AD) and studied the feudal polity and economy under the Palas, Pratiharas, and Rastrakutas (750 to 1000 AD), as well as during the two centuries preceding the establishment of the Sultanate (1000 to 1200 AD). According to Sharma, feudalism in India, unlike in Europe, began with the land grants made to learned "*brahmanas*" (the utterance of a priest, or *Brahman*. More commonly, it is used to refer to the explanation and meaning of a sacred word), temples, and monasteries, for which the epigraphic evidence begins from the 1st century AD and multiplies by the Gupta times, when villages together with their fields and inhabitants; fiscal, administrative, and judicial rights (with the right to enjoy fines received); and exemption from the interference of royal officials were given to religious beneficiaries. What was abandoned step by step to the priestly class was later given to the warrior class. Sharma (2011) postulates the existence of serfdom in Gujarat, Madhya Pradesh, Kangra, Andhra, Orissa, and Bengal during the 6th and 7th centuries on the basis of epigraphic references to the transfer of individual peasants and laborers together with the donated land. The crucial passage, in his opinion, indicates the general emergence of serfdom.

Before concluding, it is worthwhile to go through a recent research work that very elaborately analyzed the economic history of India. Deodhar (2018) "takes a comprehensive perspective on Indian economic thought leading up to Kautilya, highlighting the broader spread of economic writings prior to Kautilya as also the political economy aspects espoused by Kautilya. Thoughts on economic matters were being written in ancient Indian literature as much as the otherworldly concerns. Some of this literature, composed mostly in Sanskrit, spanned beyond a couple of millennia BCE." For example, "the *Rig Veda*, one of the premier religious texts originating in India, dates back at least to 1500 BCE (Violatti 2013). In fact, there are four different kinds of *Vedas* and most were orally composed in the third millennia BCE.

The *Arthashastra* was written as a treatise for ideal functioning of the economy, state administration, and the conduct of the ruler. Kautilya also refers to a few earlier texts from where he had improvised some of the ideas in his treatise. "Prior to the Sarasvati–Sindu epoch (2300 to 1700 BCE) and thereafter, India has had a continuous and uninterrupted existence of social, religious, and economic life, a phenomenon that finds few parallels elsewhere. While the world population was about 100 million in 1000 BCE, three-fifths of it lived in Asia, with an overwhelming number in the Indian subcontinent itself. Angus Maddison's (2003) work shows that by the 1st millennium CE, India's GDP was about one-third to half of the total world GDP. The Golden Age of India reached its peak during the Gupta dynasty (c. 6th century)" (Deodhar 2018).

The narrations of economic statements emanating from ancient Indian texts are all about worldly concerns, in contrast to the perceptions that Indians were preoccupied only with otherworldly concerns. The narration include aspects such as the pursuit of material well-being, keeping a balance between baser and otherworldly objectives, cognizance of charity as an instrument to address market failure, prudence in collection and use of taxes, bargaining, and 'verna'[5] as a means of division of labor and distributive justice. Moreover, Narada's[6] counsel to the king suggests that the grasp of economic policies of the state was also taking shape over the centuries during the 1st millennia BCE. The ideas seem to have been further developed, integrated, and presented with a definite purpose in the 4th century BCE by Kautilya in his *Arthashastra* (Deodhar 2018).

"The history of Indian economic thoughts goes back to *Vedas,* which were first composed at least three millennia ago. The expressions of early economic thoughts were grounded in the sociocultural and material environment that existed then. Though disjoint and scattered in different texts, these thoughts were profound and did get collated and improvised over the centuries. If the Sanskrit grammarian Panini came up with the nomenclature for compound interest in circa 700 BCE, it was Kautilya who understood the relation between interest rates and risk and uncertainty. In contrast, the Western world had looked down upon interest as usury until a millennium after Kautilya's treatise" Deodhar (2018). Deodhar (2018) quotes numerous verses on economics from ancient Indian texts. He also quotes various verses on how poverty was considered a bad state to be in. The original *varna* system, which degenerated into the present caste system, was invented for the division of labor. Clearly, the division of people among the four *varnas—Brahmin, Kshatriya, Vaishaya,* and *Shudra*, that is, the knowledge seeker, warrior, tradesman, and artisan/cultivator—was based on *guna-karma* (aptitude driven vocation) and not birth.

Kautilya could be considered the first preclassical economist, who in his *Arthashastra* laid down the institutional rules and regulations for the smooth functioning of the political economy exemplifying the pragmatic application of modern economics principles.

Deodhar (2018) blames foreign invasions and the British rule for scant attention paid to the history of Indian economic thought. Ancient Indian economic thought has its origins in the Vedic age. The preclassical economic thoughts that appeared in the *Vedas,* dating a millennium prior to the Greek writings, culminated in their comprehensive coverage in the *Arthashastra*, but have remained largely unnoticed. The minute details of economic principles are laid down in the *Arthashastra*.

Thapar (2002) has observed that, "in the immediate post-Gupta Period commercial activity in some parts of Northern India appears to have declined". "Declining trade in certain areas could well have been a cause. Towns became deserted when trade routes changed course and the location of markets shifted." "Urban decline could have been caused by less availability of produce for exchange. This usually consisted of manufactured items or agricultural produce such as sugarcane, cotton, and indigo, which also served rural markets. Trade would have shifted to other areas, with new towns replacing the older ones. Ports and coastal towns appear to have been less affected by the commercial decline."

"Cargoes were of goods either produced in India or brought by Indian merchants from further east. Of the items imported, silk and porcelain came from China, while China imported cotton textiles, ivory, rhinoceros horn, and a variety of precious and semiprecious stones from India. The exports westwards continued to be substantially pepper and other spices, and textiles. Mention of improved technologies in the production of cotton probably register its importance in commerce. Merchants from West Asia and the Eastern Mediterranean settled along the west coast, participating in the Indian trade with the West, and encroaching on the Eastern trade as well. Arab merchants strove to replace Indian middlemen in the trade between India, Southeast Asia, and China by going directly to these places. The North Indian overland trade with Central Asia met with vicissitudes owing to the movements of peoples such as the Turks and the Mongols" (Thapar 2002).

Endnotes

1. Economic History of India. https://www.mapsofindia.com/history/economic.html, (accessed on February 6, 2020).
2. Gupta empire economy. http://theindianhistory.org/Gupta/gupta-empire-economy.html, (accessed on December 19, 2019).
3. Agrahara was a teacher who taught courses. "An agrahara was a wider institution, a whole settlement of learned brahmans, with its own powers of government and means of maintenance granted by generous donars. The agraharas were governed by its sabha, some of whose proceedings are recorded in inscriptions". Mookerji, Radha Kumad 2016. Ancient Indian Education: Brahmanical and Buddhist, Motilal Banarsidass; 8th edition, New Delhi.
4. A monastery is a community of men or women (monks or nuns), who have chosen to withdraw from society, forming a new community devoted to religious practice. The monastery typically becomes the spiritual focus of the nearest town or village, but far enough away so as not to be disturbed during meditation.
   Buddhist Monasteries https://www.khanacademy.org/humanities/art-asia/beginners-guide-asianculture/buddhist-art-culture/a/buddhist-monasteries, (accessed on December 19, 2019).
5. Varna' defines the hereditary roots of a newborn, it indicates the colour, type, order or class of people. Four principal categories are defined: Brahmins (priests, gurus, etc.), Kshatriyas (warriors, kings, administrators, etc.), Vaishyas (agriculturalists, traders, etc., also called Vysyas), and Shudras (labourers). Each Varna propounds specific life principles to follow; newborns are required to follow the customs, rules, conduct, and beliefs fundamental to their respective Varnas.
   Caste System in Ancient India https://www.ancient.eu/article/1152/caste-system-in-ancient-india/, (accessed on December 19, 2019).
6. Narada is a Vedic sage, famous in Hindu traditions as a traveling musician and storyteller, who carries news and enlightening wisdom.

CHAPTER 2

Evolution of the Indian Economy: The Early Muslim Period and the Mughal Empire (1200 to 1760)

The Mughal Empire was a Persianate empire. "The Mughal Empire (also known as the Mogul, Timurid, or Hindustan Empire) is considered one of the classic periods of India's long and amazing history. In 1526, Zahir-ud-Din Muhammad Babur, a man with Mongol heritage from Central Asia, established a foothold in the Indian subcontinent that was to last for more than three centuries. By 1650, the Mughal Empire was one of three leading powers of the Islamic world, the so-called Gunpowder Empires, including the Ottoman Empire and Safavid Persia. At its height in about 1690, the Mughal Empire ruled almost the entire subcontinent of India, controlling four million square kilometers and a population estimated at 160 million (Szczepanski 2019a)." Babur had invaded India at the behest of Daulat Khan Lodi and won the kingdom of Delhi by defeating the forces of Ibrahim Khan Lodi at Panipat in 1526 AD. Thus, he laid the foundation of the Mughal Empire. In this chapter a broad view of the Indian economy during the rule of the Mughal emperors is analyzed under the following heads:

   I. Agriculture
  II. Industry
 III. Trade

Economy in the Medieval Period

1. **Agriculture**: The economy in Mughal Empire depended on Agriculture, trade and other Industries. Agriculture was the mainstay of the economy for a vast majority of people. It was carried on much in the same manner as today. Besides the usual crops, such as rice, wheat, barley, gram, peas, and oil seeds, *sugarcane*, indigo, and poppy were cultivated in many parts of India. There was localization of crops. *Cotton* was produced in many places of Central and Western India. Sugarcane was cultivated in parts of modern Uttar Pradesh, Bengal, and Bihar. *Indigo* was cultivated in many places of Northern and Southern India. In most cases, agricultural tools and implements were the same as now. Irrigation in the modern sense was unknown in Mughal India. The peasants usually watered their fields from the neighboring tanks and wells. Some nonagricultural products like salt and liquor were used abundantly.

   The most remarkable feature of the economic system of the Mughals was the gap that kept the producers and the consumers far asunder. The producers were agriculturists; workers in the cottage industries; artisans; producers of consumer goods like oil, cloth, sugar; and workers in the karkhanas (a manufacturing centre under state supervision during the Sultanate and Mughal periods and now a common term for a place of manufacture or assembling).

   Frequent outbreaks of famine: Agriculture depended on rainfall, and naturally, failure of seasonal rainfall or a heavy downpour resulting in flood would result in the failure of agricultural crops, which meant famine. There were frequent outbreaks of famine in Mughal India during which the sufferings of the peasants and common people would know no bounds. Bengal was visited by famine in 1575 and the Deccan and Gujarat during 1630–32. "The province of Gujarat in the northwest and the Deccan region in the central part of the empire were in political chaos due to a 2-year famine and its resulting economic depression. Toward the end of Akbar's rule (1556–1605), terrible famine began in 1595 and lasted for 3 years, affecting the same areas. During the reign of Aurangzeb, the last of the grand Mughals, there was, yet again, a 3-year famine, between 1662 and 1665, covering the same regions. Not a drop of water is reported to have fallen during these years" (Sastri and Srinivasachari 1982). A number of famines broke out during Aurangzeb's reign.

Despite from Akbar downward, the Mughal emperors tried to relieve the people's distress, but as there was no systematic effort, nor any famine policy or any easy means of transport, the relief measures were inadequate.[1]

2. **Industries**: Besides agriculture, many small industries flourished during the Mughal period. The most important small-scale industry was cotton textile and the varied industrial production by the people of India. The industrial products could not only meet the internal needs of the country but also supply the demands of the European merchants as well as merchants from different parts of Asia. Manufacture of cotton cloth was the most important industry during the period under discussion. The principal centers of cotton cloth manufacture were distributed all over the country, for instance, the Coromandel coast, Patan in Gujarat, Khandesh, Burhampur, Jaunpur, Benares, Patna, some other places in the United Provinces; Bihar; many centers in Orissa and Bengal.

The silk industry, however, was limited in scope compared with the cotton industry. It was patronized by Akbar. Bengal was the most important center of silk production and manufacture. Other centers of silk cloth manufacture were Lahore, Fatehpur Sikri, Agra, Gujarat, Benares, Bhagalpur, and Kashmir. Bengal produced silk and silk goods worth £2.5 million. Apart from silk and cotton textiles, other industries were shawl and carpet weaving, woolen goods, pottery, leather goods, and articles made of wood.

Akbar took a special interest in the development of indigenous industry. He was directly responsible for the expansion of silk weaving in Lahore, Agra, Fatehpur Sikri, and Gujarat. He opened a large number of factories at important centers, importing master weavers from Persia, Kashmir, and Turkistan. Akbar frequently visited the workshops near his palace to watch the artisans at work, which encouraged the craftsmen and raised their status. All this resulted in the establishment of a large number of shawl manufacturers in Lahore, and inducements were offered to foreign carpet weavers to settle in Agra, Fatehpur Sikri, and Lahore, and manufacture carpets to compete with those imported from Persia.

Bernier (1916) has stated that there was rigid specialization. For instance, a goldsmith would not work on silver, and the hereditary nature of the craftsmanship gave an extraordinary specialization. A weaver would weave only a particular stuff that would naturally give him a special proficiency at work through repetition. The family traditionally followed the same trade. During the 17th century and the major part of the 18th, there were extensive and diverse manufactures.

3. **Trade**: The Muslims may be divided into two major sections:
   a. Those who came with the conquerors or for trade and commerce or employment from countries like Arabia, Persia, Afghanistan, and Abyssinia
   b. The converts from the indigenous Hindu population and their descendants

As the country was open to foreign traders and travelers, there were also people of various nationalities from Europe (e.g., the Portuguese and the English) as well as Parsis and Chinese. "Sher Shah Suri during his brief reign (1538 to 1545) set a pattern that was followed by the later Mughals, especially Akbar, when he encouraged trade by linking together various parts of the country through an efficient system of roads and abolishing many inland tolls and duties. The Mughals maintained this general policy, but their rule was distinguished by the importance that foreign trade attained by the end of the 16th century. This was partly the result of the discovery of the new sea route to India, but even so, progress would have been limited if conditions within the country had not been favorable" (Columbia University n.d.).

Both Akbar and Jahāngīr interested themselves in the foreign seaborne trade, and Akbar himself took part in commercial activities for a time. The Mughals welcomed the foreign trader, provided ample protection and security for his transactions, and levied a very low custom duty (usually no more than 2.5 percent ad valorem). "Furthermore, the expansion of local handicrafts and industry resulted in a reservoir of exportable goods. Indian exports consisted mainly of manufactured articles, with cotton cloth in great demand in Europe and elsewhere. Indigo, saltpeter, spices, opium, sugar, cotton, woolen and silk cloth of various kinds, yarn, asafoetida (a fetid resinous gum obtained from the roots of a herbaceous plant, used in herbal medicine and Indian cooking), salt, beads, borax, turmeric, lac, sealing wax, and drugs of various kinds were also exported. The principal imports were bullion, horses, and a certain quantity of luxury goods for the upper classes, like raw silk, coral, amber, precious stones, superior textiles (silk, velvet, brocade, broadcloth), perfumes, drugs, Chinese goods, and European wines." (Hosmani 2014). Articles of import were sent to the towns of Lahore, Multan, Cambay, Surat, Patna, Agra, and Ahmedabad.

"By and large, however, in return for their goods, Indian merchants insisted on payment in gold or silver. Naturally, this was not popular in England and the rest of Europe. The demand for articles supplied by India was so great, however, and her requirements of European goods so limited, that Europe was obliged to trade on India's own terms until the 18th century" (Hosmani 2014). Owing to its proximity to sources of suitable timbers, Chittagong specialized in shipbuilding, and at one time supplied ships to distant Istanbul. The commercial side of the industry was in the hands of middlemen.

"In the course of time, the foreign traders established close contacts with important markets in India, and new articles that were more in demand in Western Europe began to be produced in increasing quantities. All foreign travelers speak of the wealth and prosperity of Mughal cities and large towns. The efficient system of city government under the Mughals encouraged trade. Trade and commerce developed a lot during the Mughal period" (Columbia University n.d.). There was a brisk trade with many countries of Asia and Europe. Ceylon, Burma, China, Japan, Nepal, Persia, Arabia, and Central Asia were commercially connected with India during the Mughal period. The Portuguese, the French, the Dutch, and the English purchased Indian goods for sale in European markets. In the words of Balakrishna (1954), "India was the respiratory organ for the circulation and distribution of moneys and commodities of the world; it was the sea wherein all the rivers of trade and industry flowed and thus enriched its inhabitants."

Saltpeter was manufactured in Bihar and was exported by European traders to their countries. It was used for the manufacture of gunpowder. Copper mines existed in Central India and Rajasthan. Iron was found in many parts of India. Red stone quarries were there in Rajasthan and Fatehpur. Marble came from Rajasthan. Opium, an agricultural produce, was exported after meeting internal consumption.

Maritime trade—Indian merchants versus European traders: "Aden and Moch—two leading seaports—were important commercial centers due to the influx of pilgrims and traders from Egypt who purchased Eastern products, in return for gold and silver. These ports were the main outlets of the maritime activities of the traders of Gujarat, Cambay, and Diu. The same ports were frequented by pilgrims and merchants from Lahari Bandar port in Sind, the Mughal port of Surat, the Bijapur port of Dabhol, and the Vijayanagar ports of Cannanore and Cochin".[2]

The Mughal Empire sustained a powerful agriculture- and trade-based economy along with impressive military technology. "While the emperors, nobles and *jagirdars* (Under Delhi Sultanate, the Jagirdars were allowed to collect taxes, revenues and maintain a standing army.), *mansabdars* and officers had wealth in abundance, the common people had very little of it. The economic disparity was quite evident by the standard of living, diet, dwellings, dresses, and other comforts and necessities of life. The commoners, who included the peasantry, artisans, and laborers, used to live a poor life" (Raghav 2019). People were free to choose their occupation. A very substantial portion of India's population depended on agriculture. The villages produced articles of daily use in such a way that they were able to meet their requirements. Barter system along with currency was also very popular in the rural areas. In general, it is observed that the prices of essential commodities were quite low.

4. **Land and revenue system**: The term *zamindar* connotes holders of certain rights based on revenue collection, and there are degrees of *zamindars* from those who have rights over small portions of a village upwards to the ruler of a kingdom. It goes without saying the *zamindars* were a class of intermediaries between the peasants and the state, their primary function being collection of rent. There were three main categories of intermediaries:

   i) This category comprised *zamindars* who paid tributes. These *zamindars* were rulers and often called Rajas, Raos, and so on. The tributes might be in cash or only symbolic payment by way of presentation, say, of an elephant or horse.

   ii) This category comprised *zamindars* who paid *peshkash,* that is, the revenue payable to the state. In revenue payable, the *peshkash* was also included. Ordinary *zamindars* formed the third category.

   iii) This category comprised *zamindars* who occupied a position inferior to those of the first two categories.

   The *zamindars* derived their right and title to the management of the *zamindari* from a *sanad,* which was in the nature of a contract emphasizing the obligations of the *zamindars*. Default in payment would render a *sanad* revoked. A *zamindari* might be leased out, that is, given of *ijara* (An exchange transaction applicable in Islamic regions. This is similar to a type of mortgage loan with no requirements for down payment, such as a rent-to-own arrangement in the United States.) or even sold out. With the increasing weakness of the imperial administration, there was a progressive increase in the autonomy of the *zamindars*.

   Distress of the peasant—peasants' revolt: The Mughal revenue system according to Professor Habib (2013) suffered from two infirmities. First, the revenue was set at the highest in order that the military contingents to be supplied by the *mansabdars* (Manṣabdār, member of the imperial bureaucracy of the Mughal Empire. The *manṣabdār*s governed the empire and commanded its armies in the emperor's name.) could be met out of the revenue collection of the *jagir*. Second, the revenue was fixed at so high a level that it left only the marginal surplus, that is, enough margin for the survival of the peasants, which was the barest minimum needed for their subsistence. This meant that while the appropriation of the surplus produce constituted the great wealth and the wherewithal of the Mughal imperial government to maintain its pomp and splendor as also its military strength, it left the actual producers of the wealth in a state of utter poverty.

During the early years of Aurangzeb's reign, a great portion of good cultivable land remained uncultivated for want of laborers, a large number of whom had perished due to the bad treatment and oppression of the governors, or had left the country.

In this context certain points require to be specially stressed:

i) Flight of the peasant population was a common phenomenon during the 17th century of the Mughal period.

ii) Famine was an added cause along with the oppression by the *jagirdars*, revenue farmers, and so on.

iii) Accumulation of arrears of revenue demand was another cause of absconding peasants.

Bernier (1916) has observed that "there were cases where peasantry gave up cultivation as a profession altogether." It goes without saying that the intensity of oppression varied from place to place as also due to the variance in the character of the *jagirdars* and their agents or revenue farmers.

5. **The village community**: The most outstanding feature of the Indian economy before the advent of the British was "the self-subsisting and self-perpetuating" character of the Indian villages. The village itself consumed most of the foodstuffs and other raw materials produced within itself. Its needs for handicrafts were satisfied by the artisans living within the village. The village community, within its domain, administered justice, settled land (means land, and any estate and interest therein, which was the subject of a settlement), divided occupations, and distributed the produce of the land. According to Elphinstone (2013) "these communities contained, in miniature, all the materials of a State within themselves, and were almost sufficient to protect their members if all other Government were withdrawn." The village society was composed of the cultivating class, the artisans, and the menials. Almost every village possessed a blacksmith, a potter, a barber, a washerman, a shoemaker, a weaver, and a dyer.

6. **General economic condition**: According to Pletcher (2011) "the Mughal Empire at its zenith commanded resources unprecedented in Indian history and covered almost the entire subcontinent. From 1556 to 1707, during the heyday of its fabulous wealth and glory, the Mughal Empire was a fairly efficient and centralized organization, with a vast complex of personnel, money, and information dedicated to the service of the emperor and his nobility. Much of the empire's expansion during that period was attributable to India's growing commercial and cultural contact with the outside world. The 16th and 17th centuries brought the establishment and expansion of European and non-European trading organizations in the subcontinent, principally for the procurement of Indian goods in demand abroad. Indian regions drew close to each other by means of an enhanced overland and coastal trading network, significantly augmenting the internal surplus of precious metals. With expanded connections to the wider world came also new ideologies and technologies to challenge and enrich the imperial edifice".

Prices of articles such as rice, oil, ghee, spices, vegetables, milk, meat, and livestock were very low. The people did not grovel in misery since the prices were low, although in times of natural calamities they suffered. India was quite prosperous during the time of Jahāngīr and Shah Jahan, though the foundation was laid by Akbar. He provided security and stability to the Mughal Empire. As wealth was mostly concentrated in the hands of the emperors, the nobles, the traders, and the industrialists, naturally, they led a life of pomp and pleasure. Even the common people generally did not suffer from want as almost all commodities of daily use were available at a very cheap price.

"Most of this flourishing commerce was in the hands of the traditional Hindu merchant classes, whose business acumen was proverbial. Their caste guilds added to the skills in trade and commerce that they had learned through the centuries. Not only were their disputes settled by their *panchayats* (a village council having a group of five influential older men acknowledged by the community as its governing body), but they would also frequently put pressure on the government by organized action" (Columbia University n.d.).

Bernier (1916), writing during Aurangzeb's time, declared that the Hindus possessed "almost exclusively the trade and wealth of the country." If Muslims enjoyed advantages in higher administrative posts and in the army, Hindu merchants maintained the monopoly in trade and finance that they had during the Sultanate. "Banking was almost exclusively in Hindu hands. In the years of the decline of the Mughals, a rich Hindu banker would finance his favorite rival claimant for the throne. The role of Jagat Seth of Murshidabad in the history of Bengal is well known" (Columbia University n.d.).

The individual abilities and achievements of the early Mughals—Bābur, Humāyūn, and later Akbar—largely charted this course. Bābur and Humāyūn struggled against heavy odds to create the Mughal domain, whereas Akbar, besides consolidating and expanding its frontiers, provided the theoretical framework for a truly Indian state. Picking up the thread of experimentation from the intervening Sūr dynasty (1540 to 1556), Akbar attacked narrowmindedness and bigotry, absorbed Hindus in the high ranks of the nobility, and encouraged the tradition of ruling through the local Hindu landed elites. This tradition continued until the very end of the Mughal Empire, despite the fact that some of Akbar's successors, notably Aurangzeb (1658 to 1707), had to concede to contrary forces [3]. The picture began to change with the accession of Aurangzeb. Revolts after revolts occurred that drained away the economic resources of the empire. Around the closing years of the 17th century, during Aurangzeb's rule, the economic condition of the country deteriorated. Sarkar (2009) has observed, "There appeared a great economic impoverishment of India." "The Mughal Empire began to collapse under its own weight. In 1707, when Aurangzeb died, serious threats from the peripheries had begun to accentuate the problems at the core of the empire". [4]

7. **The Mughals' contributions**: The Mughals came to India as conquerors but lived in the subcontinent as Indians, not colonizers. They merged their identity as well as that of their group with India and the two became inseparable, giving rise to an enduring culture and history. Akbar onwards, all Mughals were born in India, with

many having Rajput mothers, and their "Indianness" was complete (Mukhia 2004).

As regards India's economic status prior to her becoming a British colony, the Cambridge historian Maddison (2007) has stated that India had the world's largest economy in the 1st century and 11th century. The percentage of growth defined, with 32.9 percent in the 1st century which declined to 28.9 percent in the 10 AD and registered further decline in 17 AD with 24.5 percent. But there was no economic growth. It was during 1000 to 1500 AD that India began to see economic growth, with its highest (20.9 percent GDP growth rate) being under the Mughals.

Before the Europeans, India was ruled for over 700 years by the Mughal emperors and had some of the most powerful rulers who had good knowledge of trade and commerce. India was better economically during these times and saw some of the most golden years in terms of its economy. Till the 17th century, India was not totally under the rule of the British, and hence, it was not yet plundered by these colonial rulers. According to Dutt (1963), the doyen of historians, "India in the eighteenth century was a great manufacturing as well as a great agricultural country."

It is established now that the Mughals did not take away money. They invested in infrastructure, in building great monuments that are a local and tourist draw, generating crores of rupees annually. A beautiful new style known as "Indo-Islamic architecture" that imbibed the best of both sensibilities was born. They invested in local arts and crafts, and encouraged old and created new skill sets in India. As Swapna Liddle (the convener of The Indian National Trust for Art and Cultural Heritage (INTACH') Delhi Chapter says,

> To my mind the greatest Mughal contribution to India was in the form of patronage to the arts. Whether it was building, artisanal crafts like weaving and metalworking, or fine arts like painting, they set standards of taste and perfection that became an example for others to follow, and brought India the global recognition for high quality handmade goods that it still enjoys.[5]

Mughal paintings, jewels, arts, and crafts are the key possessions of many a Western museum and gallery as they were looted in and after 1857. Some can be found in Indian museums too. Art and literature flourished under the Mughal Empire. Frances W Pritchett, professor emerita, Columbia University (n.d.) says, "The greatness of the Mughals consisted in part at least in the fact that the influence of their court and government permeated society, giving it a new measure of harmony."[6] Almost all Mughal emperors either themselves or the scholars of their court wrote about contemporary life. "The Mughals had encouraged trade by developing roads, river transport, sea routes, ports and abolishing many inland tolls and taxes. Indian handicrafts were developed. There was a thriving export trade in manufactured goods such as cotton cloth, spices, indigo, woolen and silk cloth, salt, and so on. A very efficient system of administration set up by Akbar facilitated an environment of trade and commerce. It was this that led the East India Company to seek trade concessions from the Mughal Empire and eventually control and then destroy it".[7]

During the Medieval period, which had its start from 8th century and continued up to the 18th century, rulers like Ala-u-din Khilji, Mohammad Bin Tuglaque, Ferozshah, Shershah, and Akbar introduced certain measures for economic reforms for the uplift of the Indian economy. Among such measures, the land reform and revenue reform measures of Shershah, and the revenue reforms and other economic reforms of Akbar were remarkable. But most of the Indian kings and queens of the medieval period were very much preoccupied with immaterial objects at the cost of material objects, totally leading toward the unnecessary wastage of resources. For example, Jehangir (1569–1627) was interested in art, literature, and architecture and the Mughal gardens in Srinagar remain an enduring testimony to his artistic taste. He married Mehr-un-Nisa whom he gave the title of Nur Jahan (light of the world). He loved her with blind passion and handed over the complete reins of administration to her.

Thus, after Kautilya, near about 2,000 years passed without having any serious development in terms of Indian economic thought.[8] Table 2.1 gives a rough indication of the social structure of the Moghul Empire.

Table 2.1 Social structure of the Moghul Empire

Percentage of labor force		Percentage of national income after tax
18	NONVILLAGE ECONOMY	52
1	Moghul Emperor and Court *Mansabdars* *Jagirdars* Native princes Appointed *zamindars* Hereditary *zamindars*	15
17	Merchants and bankers Traditional professions Petty traders and entrepreneurs Soldiers & petty bureaucracy Urban artisans & construction workers Servants Sweepers Scavengers	37
72	**VILLAGE ECONOMY**	45
	Dominant castes Cultivators and rural artisans Landless laborers Servants Sweepers Scavengers	
10	**TRIBAL ECONOMY**	3

Source: Maddison (2006).

8. **End of the Mughals**: "The Mughal Empire was unprepared to deal with the threat posed by European intruders. It failed to maintain its military superiority. It imploded from within, as the emperors spent more time choosing which gorgeous costume to wear than they did attending to governance. They failed to learn the lesson, and after a positive, prosperous start allowed their empire to deteriorate, losing its commercial edge and literally eating up its wealth." "By the mid-19th century, the British were controlling vast tracts of the Mughal Empire and other principalities through a series of treaties and alliances. Technically, they still ruled as agents of the Mughal Empire, but were in practice exercising complete power." "Under what was called the "Lahore policy," the British annexed any state over which they

exercised influence if they considered its ruler decadent or if he did not have an heir whom they were willing to recognize".[9]

Added to all this was the cruel treatment of the weavers and traders, which hastened the decline of the Indian trading community and the destruction of the manufactures. The political disintegration of the Mughal Empire sapped India's economic vitality. External invasion and internal disruption affected the easy transit of goods from one part of the country to the other. Interprovincial trade gradually came to a standstill. What still lingered was due to the fact that the Mughal Empire took some length of time to die. When it became incapacitated, the economic reins were assumed by the English merchant community.

"Queen Victoria was declared Empress of India, and Britain assumed direct control of its Indian possessions, winding up the East India Company. They argued that Indians were unable to govern themselves properly, and continued their annexation policy, removing "corrupt" Indian princes on a regular basis. India became the jewel in the British Empire." "By the early 20th century, the whole of the subcontinent, including Sri Lanka, was under British administration, although many princely states remained theoretically independent."[10] The advent of the European trading communities and the eventual supremacy of the English in the matter carried with it also the subjugation of Indian trade and industries and conversion of India into a raw material producing and supplying country. All this had its impact on the Indian trading community.

Ali (2003) has "highlighted an interesting ongoing debate as to whether the Mughal Empire had a middle class and so possessed the potential to develop into a capitalist economy. It has been argued that such was the case. Leonard (1979) has even tried to apply the "Great Firm" theory to explain the decline of the Mughal Empire. Essentially, proponents of the theory point to the development of commerce, banking and the existence of large professional classes. Opponents of the thesis include Irfan Habib (2013), who has argued that the Mughal urban economy and commerce rested heavily on the system of land tax extraction and was incapable of independent development into capitalism."

Table 2.2 Timeline of the Mughal Dynasty

Sl. No.	Mughal ruler	Period of rule
1.	Babur	1526–1530
2.	Humayun	1530–1540, 1555–1556
3.	Akbar	1556–1605
4.	Jahangir	1605–1627
5.	Shah Jahan	1627–1658
7.	Aurangzeb	1658–1707
8.	Bahadur Shah	1707–1712
9.	Jahandar Shah	1712–1713
10.	Furrukhsiyar	1713–1719
11.	Rafi ul–Darjat	1719–1719
12.	Nikusiyar	1719–1743
11.	Mohammed Ibrahim	1720–1744
14.	Mohammed Shah	1719–1720, 1720–1748
15.	Ahmad Shah Bahadur	1748–1754
16.	Alamgir II	1754–1759
17.	Shah Jahan III	1759–1759
18.	Shah Alam II	1759–1806
19.	Akbar Shah II	1806–1837
20.	Bahadur Shah II	1837–1857

Source: Timeline of the Mughal Dynasty. https://www.worldatlas.com/articles/timeline-of-the-mughal-dynasty.html
Note: **Contemporary use:** In popular news jargon, Mughal or Mogul denotes a successful business magnate who has built for himself a vast (and often monopolistic) empire in one or more specific industries. The usage seems to have an obvious reference to the expansive and wealthy empires built by the Mughal emperors in India.[11]

Endnotes

1. Social, Economic and Cultural History of the Medieval Age. http://www.historydiscussion.net/history-of-india/social-economic-and-cultural-history-of-the-medieval-age/5917, (accessed on December 23, 2019).

2. Ibid.

3. Encyclopædia Britannica. n.d. "The Mughal Empire, 1526–1761." https://www.britannica.com/place/India/The-Mughal-Empire-1526-1761, (accessed on December 23, 2019).

4. Aurangzeb. https://www.britannica.com/place/India/Aurangzeb, (accessed on December 23, 2019).

5. Safvi, R. 2018. If Mughals Did Not Loot India, What Exactly Was Their Contribution to India? Unlike the British, They Did Not Colonise the Subcontinent. https://www.dailyo.in/variety/rajputs-mughal-empire-india-economy-medieval-india-british-raj-1857-revolt/story/1/21997.html, (accessed on December 23, 2019).

6. Ibid.

7. Sone Ki Chidiya: India ranked above US, UK, China, Japan in Mughal era. https://m.dailyhunt.in/news/india/english/the+siasat+daily+english-epaper-siaseten/sone+ki+chidiya+india+ranked+above+us+uk+china+japan+in+mughal+era-newsid-90562748, (accessed on December 23, 2019).

8. Economics Discussion. n.d. Evolution of Indian Economy. http://www.economicsdiscussion.net/indian-economy/evolution-of-indian-economy/18999, (accessed on December 23, 2019).

9. Mughal Empire. https://courses.lumenlearning.com/atd-tcc-worldciv2/chapter/mughal-empire/, (accessed on December 23, 2019).

10. New World Encyclopedia. 2018. "Mughal Empire." https://www.newworldencyclopedia.org/entry/Mughal_Empire.

11. Ibid.

CHAPTER 3

Indian Economy during the British Regime (1761 to 1947)

The English East India Company established its supremacy in Bengal in 1757, and it was a century later, in 1858, when the Crown took over the administration of India. Subsequently, British Crown rule over India lasted 90 years, from 1858 to 1947.

Advent of the British (1600 to 1740): Encyclopedia Britannica in its narrative has provided a very lucid description of the period between 1600 to 1740 and we are tempted to use their narrative in detail for this section. It has stated that "the English expedition to India was entrusted to the (English) East India Company, which received its monopoly rights of trade in 1600. The company included a group of London merchants attracted by Eastern prospects. Its objective was to trade in spices, and it was at first modestly organized on a single-voyage basis. These separate voyages were initially financed by groups of merchants within the company, and in 1657, a permanent joint stock company was established. The company's objective was to procure the spices of the East Indies, and it went to India only for the secondary purpose of securing cotton for sale to the spice growers".

It further explained that "in India, the English found the Portuguese enjoying Mughal recognition at the Western Indian port of Surat. Portuguese command of the sea nullified the English embassy to the Mughal court in spite of its countenance by the emperor Jahāngīr. However, the English victory at Swally Hole in 1612 over the Portuguese, whose control of the pilgrim sea route to Mecca was resented by the Mughals, brought a dramatic change. The embassy of Sir Thomas Roe

(1615 to 1618) to the Mughal court secured an accord (in the form of a *farmān*, or grant of privileges) by which the English secured the right to trade and to establish factories in return for becoming the virtual naval auxiliaries of the empire. This success determined that India, not the Far East, should be the chief theatre of English activity in Asia" (Encyclopedia Britannica).

It went on to express in following words "there followed through the 17th century a period of peaceful trading through factories operating under Mughal grants. This held good for Surat and later for Hugli (1651) in Bengal. In the south the factory at Masulipatam (1611) was moved to the site of Madras (now Chennai), granted by a Hindu raja (1640); it shortly (1647) came under the control of the sultans of Golconda and thence passed to the Mughals in 1687. The only exception to this arrangement was the island port of Bombay (now Mumbai); although independently held, its trade was small because the Marathas, soon locked in combat with the Mughals, held the hinterland."

"The trade the company developed was a trade in bulk instead of in highly priced luxury goods; the profits were a factor of volume rather than scarcity; it worked in competitive instead of monopolistic conditions; and it depended upon political goodwill instead of intimidation. But despite being profitable, it encountered difficulties as well. The Indians would take little other than silver in exchange for their goods, and the export of bullion was anathema to the concept of mercantilism, then England's reigning political economy. Lack of military power meant management of Asian governments instead of their coercion. Lack of home dominance meant compromise and hazard of fortune."

"To solve the silver problem, the English developed a system of country trade, the profits of which helped to pay for the annual investment of goods for England. Madras and Gujarat supplied cotton goods, and Gujarat supplied indigo as well; silk, sugar, and saltpeter (for gunpowder) came from Bengal, while there was a spice trade along the Malabar Coast from 1615 on a competitive basis with the Dutch and Portuguese. Opium was shipped to East Asia, where it later became the basis of the Anglo-Chinese tea trade. The merchants lived in factories (trading houses) or in a collegiate type of settlement where life was confined, colorful, and often short."

The Encyclopedia Britannica has pointed out the difficulties which the East India Company was facing in England.

By way of concluding this section we would like to quote again Encyclopedia Britannica "a way for rivals to harass the company was to limit the sale of cotton goods in England. In India the company suffered a serious setback when it resolved to resort to armed trade and to attack the Mughals. Out of this fiasco came both the foundation of Calcutta (now Kolkata) by Job Charnock in 1690—a mudflat that had the advantage of a deep anchorage—and the age of fortified factories surrounded by satellite towns. These were the answers, with Mughal consent, to increasing Indian insecurity. The Madras factory was already fortified, and Fort William in Calcutta followed in 1696. The company thus had, with independent Bombay, three centers of Indian power".

"For the next half century the company confined its relations with the Mughals. Fresh privileges were obtained in Delhi, and these they were content to argue about rather than fight for. The factors were learning the art of Indian diplomacy as they had formerly to learn the arts of Indian commercial management" (Encyclopedia Britannica).

The Extension of British Power (1760 to 1856)

The European and the British traders initially came to India for trading purposes. Around the 18th Century a number of significant events took place in the world. One such event was the Industrial Revolution which took place in England. It gradually spread to other countries of Europe also. *With the discovery of new sea and trade routes a Portuguese called Vasco da Gama discovered India in 1498. As a result, the English, French, Portuguese and the Dutch came to India for trade.* At the same time, they also required a market to sell their finished goods. India provided such a platform to Britain to fulfill all their needs. The 18th century was a period of internal power struggle in India and with the declining power of the Mughal Empire, the British officials were provided with the perfect opportunity to establish their hold over Indian Territory. They did these through numerous wars, forced treaties, annexations of and alliances with the various regional powers all over the country. Their new administrative and economic policies helped them consolidate their control over the country. Ellis (2017) has pointed out that in 1764, Mīr Qāsim, the son-in-law of the Nawab of Bengal, Mir Jāfar, was defeated at the Battle of Buxar (Baksar). This conflict, rather than the famous one at Plassey, was the decisive battle that gave Bengal to the British. Robert Clive, who returned to Bengal in May 1765 and turned the whole Mughal Empire into a company-sponsored state. In 1765, the Mughal Emperor granted the Company the diwani (the right to harvest the revenues of Bengal, Bihar and Orissa), which provided funds to bolster the Company's military presence in the sub-continent. Further territorial acquisitions in India during the late 18th and early nineteenth centuries cemented the change in the Company's role from mere trader to a hybrid sovereign power.

"Clive's next step was to settle Bengal's status. The Mughal emperor still had much influence, though little power. Clive's solution was to ob-tain from Shah 'Ālam, the "dewanee," or revenue-collecting power, in Bengal and Bihar." "The nawab was left in charge of the judiciary and magistracy, but he was helpless because he had no army and could get money to raise one only from the company".

"This was Clive's system of "dual government." The actual administra-tion remained in Indian hands". "The company, acting in the name of the emperor and using Indian personnel and the traditional apparatus of government, now ruled Bengal. Within the company, Clive enforced his authority by accepting some resignations and enforcing others. Clive left Calcutta in February 1767. His work—diplomatic, political, and administrative—was a beginning rather than a complete settlement. But in each direction, instead of looking back to the past, it reached out to the future" Ellis (2017).

The Company Bahadur: "The year 1765, when Clive arrived in India, can be said to mark the real beginning of the British Empire in India as a territorial dominion." However, "the structure of the administration was Mughal, not British, and its operators were Indian. It was a con-tinuation of the traditional state, but under British control, and it can be aptly described by the company's popular title, the Company Bahadur, which meant the "valiant" or honorable company. Lord Cornwallis (governor-general, 1786 to 1793 and 1805) substituted largely British for

Indian personnel. The revenue was collected by the officers of the deputy nawab; and the language of administration was Persian. Only the army broke with the past, with its British officers, its discipline, and its Western organization and tactics" Ellis (2017).

"It was this state that Warren Hastings inherited when he became governor of Bengal in 1772. Noteworthy in his 13-year rule were his internal administration, his dealings with his council, and his foreign policy. Hastings was armed with authority by the directors, substituted British for Indian collectors working under a Board of Revenue. The change gave legal power to those who already wielded it, and in the future their irregularities could more easily be dealt with than could the surreptitious dealings through the old Indian collectors. Finally, Hastings instituted a network of civil and criminal courts in place of the deputy *nawabs*. The same law was administered by British judges, who were often incompetent, but a model was provided into which Western ideas and practices could later be fed. These changes held good through the period of Hastings' rule and may be said to have provided a viable, though not yet very competent or equitable, state" Ellis (2017).

The Company and the State: The British Parliament decided to place a curb on the Company's autonomy. From 1784 the Board of Control supervised the East India Company's (EIC) administrative and political affairs, but not its' commercial business nor the exercise of patronage by the directors. The Company's mercantile monopoly came increasingly under attack and its commercial operations were at first scaled down by Parliament after years of pressure from the free trade lobby and then wound up completely by the Charter Act of 1833. The Company continued in its imperial role until 1858 when, in the aftermath of the military and civil rebellion in the north of the sub-continent, the Government of India Act transferred its powers to the India Office, a department of state. The EIC was finally dissolved on 1 June 1874, after shareholders received compensation from Parliament.[1]

"In India a governor-generalship of Fort William in Bengal was established by the British government, with supervisory control over the other Indian settlements and Warren Hastings as its first incumbent. Hastings was given four named councilors, but future appointments were to be made by the company. A supreme court with a chief justice and three judges was also set up. All of this was achieved as a result of the Regulating Act, passed in 1773, which was a first step toward taking the political direction of British India out of the hands of the company and of securing a unified overall control. Ten years later, Prime Minister William Pitt's India Act proved to be the next landmark decision in this regard, because it gave the British government control of policy without patronage. By the enforcement of the provisions of this Act, the company slowly became a managing agency of the British government" (Encyclopedia Britannica).

The ascent to paramountcy: The "term of office of the governor-general Wellesley (1798 to 1805) was a decisive period in the rise of the British dominion. During his governance, the company undertook to protect a state from external attack in return for control of its foreign relations." Thus, Wellesley's work, avowedly imperialistic, made ultimate supremacy of the British inevitable.

In the course of the next few decades, The year 1818 marks a watershed, when the British Empire in India became the British Empire of India. Control of India was given to a British Governor-General, who reported back to the British Parliament. It should be noted that the British Raj included only about two-thirds of modern India, with the other portions under the control of local princes. However, Britain exerted great pressure on these princes, effectively controlling all of India (Szczepanski 2019b). **The diplomatic settlement of 1818**, except for a few annexations before 1857, remained in force until 1947. "Given the fact of expansion, Britain enjoyed the advantage of overseas reinforcement through its sea power and of reserves of power, far greater than that of any Indian prince, through its rapidly expanding industrial economy. Then there were the technical advantages of arms and military discipline and the immense general advantage of a disciplined civilian morale" (Encyclopedia Britannica).

Organization and economic policy in British India: The land revenue was fixed permanently. In Bengal, among the other reforms that he had instituted, Cornwallis's permanent settlement of the land revenue was the measure that most deeply affected the life and structure of Indian society, three-quarters of the revenue coming from the land. The "settlement" was the decision in 1793 to stabilize the revenue demand at a fixed annual figure, with a commission to the *zamindar* for collection, and to regard him as the owner of his *zamindari*. The net result of this measure was the creation of a landlord class, loyal to the British connection but divorced from touch with the cultivators of their lands. The government, receiving the revenue from the *zamindars*, knew little of the people and could do little for them. This was the arrangement made under the Permanent settlement that was introduced in Bengal and Bihar in 1793.

"At first the Bengal system was thought to provide the key to Indian administration, but doubts multiplied with the years. In Madras, Sir Thomas Munro retained the paternal framework of the government but introduced a radically differing method of revenue management known as the *ryotwari* system, in which the settlement was made directly with the cultivator, each field being separately measured and annually assessed. This system eliminated the middleman but sometimes placed the cultivators at the mercy of lower officials, who often formed cliques of caste groups. In Western India, the *ryotwari* method was used for assessing land revenue, which was collected through local officials from the village headmen. In the north, it was the largely autonomous village system with its joint ownership and cultivation by caste oligarchies." According to Pletcher (2011) "the resulting system of administration of British India was still largely Indian in pattern, though it was now British in direction and superintendence. It was paternalistic and hierarchical in nature". "The British established on a national scale the idea of property in land, and the resulting buying and selling caused large class changes. Their new security benefitted the commercial classes generally, but the deliberate sacrifice of Indian industry to the claims of the new machine industries of Britain ruined such ancient crafts as cotton and silk weaving. The new legal system, with its network of courts, proved efficient on the criminal justice side but was heavily overloaded on the civil side".

"The real breakthrough in terms of the future direction of British governance in India came with the governor-generalship of Lord William Bentinck (1828 to 1835) and with the Whig government, that from 1830 carried the great Reform Bill. It was as a social reformer that Bentinck made the most indelible mark on the future of India" (Encyclopedia

Britannica). "This period saw the British in India committed to promoting the positive welfare of India instead of merely holding a ring for trade and exploitation; to introducing Western knowledge, science, and ideas alongside the Indian with a view to eventual absorption and adoption; and to the promotion of Indian participation in the government with a view to eventual Indian self-government. It was the changeover from the concept of a Mughal successor state—the Company Bahadur—to that of a Westernized self-governing dominion. In the former case, the British were wardens of a stationary society; in the latter, trustees of an evolving one." Pletcher (2011).

Economic effects: India became an economic colony of Industrial England. With the coming of industrialization in England, the textile industry there made important headway. There was now a reverse of the direction of textile trade between Britain and India. There was a massive import of machine made clothes from English factories to Indian markets. This import of large amount of products manufactured by mechanical looms in England led to increase threat for the handicraft industries as the British goods were sold at a much cheaper price. India was then, mainly agricultural, and its industries, though significant, were marginal to its whole economy. The latter changed, however, with the acquisition of Bengal. The bias in favor of British merchants diverted trade from their Indian counterparts. The British had come to India with the idea of making immense profits. This meant buying of raw materials at very cheap rates and selling finished goods at much higher prices. The British succeeded in selling their goods at a cheap price as foreign goods were given free entry in India without paying any duty. On the other hand, Indian handicrafts were taxed heavily when they were sent out of the country. Besides, under the pressure of its industrialists, British government often imposed a protective tariff on Indian textiles. Therefore, within a few years, India from being an exporter of clothes became an exporter of raw cotton and an importer of British clothes. This reversal made a huge impact on the Indian handloom weaving industry leading to its virtual collapse. This steadily undermined the Indian handicraft industries until all but the highest and coarsest grades of cloth were squeezed out. The district of Dacca (now Dhaka, Bangladesh) was especially illustrative of this process. It also created unemployment for a large community of weavers.

The "permanent settlement (1793), after an initial period of dislocation, gave relief and security to the *zamindars* in Bengal, though not to the cultivators of their lands. In Madras, economic settlement turned on the working of the *ryotwari* revenue system; regularity of collection was offset by the severity of assessment, and the same may be said of both Western and Northern India" (Encyclopedia Britannica). Western inventions like the telegraph, modern irrigation, railways, and steamships followed, throwing India open to the industrial mechanistic and democratic world.

Social effects: The social effects of this period were considerable. They mainly took the form of the displacement of classes. In Bengal, the social link between landholder and cultivator had been broken, with a cash nexus replacing traditional rights. The British wanted the Indians to be educated and modern enough to consume their goods but not to the extent that it proved detrimental to British interests. They wanted India to be a part of the modern, progressive world of science. British brought ideas of freedom, equality, liberty and human rights to India and resulted in to changes in condition of Indian women, education and reform movement. As such, during British rule Indian society underwent many changes.

Cultural effects: The cultural effects of British influence during the century from 1757 to 1857, though less spectacular, were in the long run farther-reaching. Educating the Indians in British modes of thought and stamping out cultural practices such as sati—the practice of immolating a widow on the death of her husband. The British thought of their rule as a form of "autocratic paternalism". The British also created "divide and rule" policies, pitting Hindu and Muslim Indians against one another. In 1905, the colonial government divided Bengal into Hindu and Muslim sections; this division was revoked after strong protests. Britain also encouraged the formation of the Muslim League of India in 1907 (Szczepanski 2019b).

In British India, land settlements had produced much social dislocation while purporting to respect traditional rights and to learn from the past; in particular, the Western concept of property in land had led to much social displacement. The Westernized legal system was efficient in suppressing crime but dilatory in upholding rights and incomprehensible for most natives in its working.

The revolutionary aspect of the British presence was the decision to introduce Western knowledge and science through the medium of the English language. Along with education came the Christian missionary intrusion, with its moral and ideological challenge (Encyclopedia Britannica).

Economic policy and development (1858–1947): British rule in India formally lasted between 1858 and 1947 (Roy 2002).

According to Roy (2016) "interpretations of the role of the state in economic change in colonial (1858 to 1947) and post-colonial India (1947) tend to presume that the colonial was an exploitative state, while the post-colonial was a developmental state. However, the differences between the two states lay elsewhere than in the drive to exploit Indian resources by a foreign power. The difference was that British colonial policy was framed with reference to global market integration, whereas post-colonial policy was framed with reference to nationalism".

The fate of the Indian economy under British rule has long been a battleground of historiography, with little agreement between historians, either of interpretation or of fact. This partly reflects the difficulties of the sources, but also the widely differing expectations, assumptions, and "counter-factual" models. It is emphasized that concepts of "development" be situated in their time-bound historical contexts and construed in relation to political and social, as well as narrowly economic, criteria (Washbrook 2012).

Endnote

1. A Brief History of the English East India Company 1600–1858. https://www.qdl.qa/en/brief-history-english-east-india-company-1600%E2%80%931858, (accessed on December 24, 2019).

CHAPTER 4

Impact of the British Regime on the Indian Economy

In this chapter an overview of the way in which the British restructured the indigenous economic system of India, a British colony, to suit their objective of maximum exploitation is presented. Colonization is described as "governance of a land and its people, now on behalf of and primarily for the economic benefits of a community of people inhabiting a far-off land" (Mukhia 2004). The 17th century and the first few decades of the 18th century were bright both for Indian trade and traders. But the process of drainage of the Indian economy started with the growing commercial power of the English and with the gradual transformation of the East India Company into a political power in the post-Plassey period. Indian trade and traders began to suffer till the latter were eventually ousted from the field due to unfair competition from the English. The invasion of the English into the private trade of the country, their abuse of *dastaks* (a trade permit sanctioned to the east India company by the Mughal government), among others, had the effect of eliminating the Indian merchants from the playing field. The scramble for riches and the scandalous misuse of *dastaks* after the Battle of Plassey unleashed the forces of economic decline and saw the emergence of the commercial and political supremacy of the English.

The objective of the East India Company was to import raw materials from India, process them, and export the products to earn revenue. This resulted in India being an exporter of goods of less value and an importer of manufactured goods of higher value, which made the nation's economy spiral downwards. One of the principles of the British commercial policy in India was to protect the textile industry of Britain against the competition of the Indian textile manufacturers. An Act was passed in 1700 prohibiting the use of silk goods and calico prints from Bengal, Persia, China, and the East Indies in England. However, raw silk was allowed to be imported into England in 1701.

The development of nationalism and a political consciousness at the turn of the century made Indian scholars keenly aware of the economic exploitation of India by the British, which formed the theme of the writings of Naoroji (1902) and Dutt (1963). The strong nationalist movement that followed the partition of Bengal in 1905 gave a great impetus to the study of the economic conditions of ancient India. The period between 1916 and 1925, coinciding with the postwar nationalist and revolutionary movements sweeping across Europe and Asia, marked the peak of the nationalist movement in India as well.

Indian scholars focused on analyzing the problems of poverty and colonialism prevailing in the country during those days. Dadabhai Naoroji (1825 to 1917), Mahadev Govind Ranade (1866 to 1915), and Romesh Chunder Dutt (1848 to 1919) analyzed the problem of poverty in India from new perspectives. Naoroji, in 1902, wrote a detailed analysis on the exploitation of the Indian economy by the British regime and advocated for popular protectionism. He was also the first person in India who made an estimate of national income in India, personally putting in his effort in doing so.

Ranade (2018) also criticized the free trade policy followed in India and reflected colonial light in the system of international division of labor. He realized the influence of various psychological and institutional factors on the economic development of India. Ranade's contribution to economic thought was a synthesis of the British policy of free trade and colonialism and some other ideas of the German school of thought. After Ranade, Dutt undertook a detailed analysis of the "drain theory" of Naoroji. These Indian economists of the 19th century had realized that the economic problems of India were undeniably connected with British colonialism.

Prior to British colonial rule, India was well known for its handicraft industries dealing with cotton and silk textiles, metal and precious stone-work, etc. These products manufactured in India had a worldwide market due to the fine quality of the materials used and high standards of craftsmanship employed in the exported products. Gadgil (1938) attributed the decline in handicrafts in India to the following three factors:

I. the disappearance of the court culture of late Mughal days and old aristocracy;

II. the establishment of an alien rule with the influx of many foreign influences that such a change in the nature of government meant; and

III. competition from machine-made goods.

For the purpose of precise presentation, the period has been divided into three broad stages of British colonialism in India. They are as under[1]:

I. **Mercantile development (1757 to 1813)**: "The East India Company began to use its political power to monopolize the trade in India. It dictated the terms of trade in its dealings with the traders and merchants of Bengal. The Company imposed inflated prices of goods leading to adventurous capitalism whereby the wealth was created by the political clout of the British traders. The revenue collected from Bengal was used to finance exports to England".

II. **Industrial phase (1813 to 1858)**: "With the development of British industries, India was exploited by its colonial masters as a market for British goods. With the passing of the Act of 1813, only one-way trade was allowed by the British, as a result of which, the Indian markets were flooded with cheap, machine-made imports from newly industrialized Britain. This led to the loss of both the Indian and foreign markets for traders in the country. Now, Indians were forced to export their raw materials to Britain and import finished goods from there. The British traders imposed heavy import duties on the Indian products exported to England in order to discourage them from being consumed in the British market".

III. **Financial phase (1860 onwards)**: "After the British consolidated their position in India, they converted India into a market for British manufacturers while still being a supplier of foodstuffs and raw materials. In the second half of the 19th century, modern machine-based industries started coming up in India, helped by the introduction of the railways in 1853, and the post and telegraph later in the same year. There was a rush of foreign investment in India, with investors mainly lured by the chances of high profits and the availability of cheap labor and raw materials. The banking system was introduced in the form of the Avadh Commercial Bank in 1881. Homegrown industries also came into existence, such as Tata Iron and Steel in 1907. Socially, this led to the rise of an industrial capitalist class and the working class became a very important feature of this phase" of Indian economic growth.

The colonial era had a tremendous impact on the economy due to the changes in the process of taxation, trade, property taxes, etc., all of which resulted in the breakdown of the economy, and which also caused the composition of agricultural produce to change drastically.

The Changing Narrative of India's Economic History

Roy (2002) in his study observed that "until quite recently, most economic history research in India was conducted within a paradigm that saw development and underdevelopment, industrialization and deindustrialization, as two sides of the same coin. This formulation pervaded both Indian nationalist thought as well as leftist historiography". This view was first challenged when Morris (1963) proposed a more positive view of 19th-century Indian development. The main message was that economic growth in 19th-century India was constrained by productive capacity rather than by politics, which played a benign or positive role. Irrespective of the difference in their political status, British and Indian economic fortunes were complementary rather than contradictory. The uses and benefits of public goods, such as the railways or the telegraph, were not restricted to ethnic groups and benefitted all equally.

Regarding the colonial rule, questions have been raised as to how large, of what nature, and how lasting the impact was. These questions have long guided the study of the economic history of India. The imperialist, or "orientalist," belief was that the empire heralded modernity in India, while 20th-century writers on imperialism and development believed in an enduring link between colonialism and underdevelopment. Scholarship continues along the imperialism–underdevelopment axis, but this stance looks increasingly dated and disoriented, especially at a time when economic liberalization in India is drawing upon the tenets of classical political economy on which British policy in India was founded. Roy (2002) argues that "a different narrative of Indian economic history is needed. An exclusive focus on colonialism as the driver of India's economic history misses those continuities that arise from economic structures or local conditions. In fact, market-oriented British imperial policies did initiate a process of economic growth based on the production of goods that were intensive in labor and natural resources. However, the productive capacity per worker was constrained by the low rates of private and public investment in infrastructure". The paragraphs that follow are largely based on the research analysis of Roy (2002). It is useful to focus on three major features during the period of British colonial rule:

I. *Structural features* include the overwhelming importance of natural resources and labor to economic growth, fluctuations, and welfare. Agriculture and labor-intensive industry and services were the main livelihoods throughout this period and beyond.

II. *Global features* focus on the fact that India's economy was more open during this period compared with periods before and after colonialism. India participated in a global revolution in transport and communication, which include especially the opening of the Suez Canal, and the introduction of the railways, and the telegraph.

III. *Colonial features* indicate India's status as a colony imposed certain peculiarities on its balance of payments, like large remittances paid by the government to Britain. However, the ratio of investment to government expenditure was apparently much higher in British India than in earlier Mughal India.

The structural features of India's economy changed slowly. For example, India's economy was primarily agrarian before, during, and since colonialization. By 1757, the English East India Company commanded political power in Bengal. This transition from trade to direct rule can be explained partly by the needs of the trade itself. British mercantilists criticized Britain's payment of bullion for Indian textiles, the most important item in this trade. Local political circumstances that enabled the British to command the land revenues of Bengal came as a less controversial means of payment. The local circumstances included the support of the elite disaffected by the local rulers. When the company's monopoly in trade ended in the early 19th century, it was committed to building an empire. By 1857, the boundaries of colonial India, which were the basis on which two nations were carved out in 1947, had been defined.

A more or less uniform administrative system came into place in this time span. In the economic sphere, there were several major changes. Agrarian "settlements," which were contracts between the state and the cultivators on property rights and revenue commitments, were drawn. The British wanted to create a class of cultivators with secure property rights who would yield more revenue to them by pursuing profit-oriented cultivation.

Another set of changes had their origin in foreign trade in an increasingly integrated world where trade expanded quickly. Indian exports had been dominated by textile manufacturers in the 18th century. The composition of exports changed to non-manufactured goods and that of imports to manufactured goods, notably British textiles. The early 19th century saw the rise of new commodities in trade, such as indigo, opium, and cotton. The profits of these trades sustained new commercial-cum-port towns, such as Calcutta, Bombay, and Madras. There is a widely shared belief that the consolidation of British power in the economic sphere saw a violent and uncompensated economic disturbance. The fact that there was such a decline, the period in which it happened, the regions affected, and the causes behind it remain imprecise. One thing is clear—India's traditional cotton textile industry declined between 1820 and 1860. First, an export market for Indian cloth disappeared. Later, handspun cotton yarn and hand-woven cloth suffered due to the import of yarn and cloth from the mills in England. The decline seems dramatic if seen against India's earlier dominance in the world textile trade. This single example of decay appears to have generated the "deindustrialization" thesis, which at its narrowest holds that early British rule introduced a violent shock to India's economy, and at its broadest holds that colonialism caused underdevelopment. Roy (2002) has stated that both the narrow and broad inferences, however, are deeply questionable for a number of reasons:

I.   The industrial decline was apparently restricted to cotton textiles.

II. The decline of the textile industry did not continue through the rest of the 19th century and on into the 20th century as British colonial rule strengthened, which calls into question whether the fundamental cause was the rise of colonial rule in the first place.

III. A decline in cotton textiles was not capable of causing economy-wide distress. The proportion of textile export in total textile production was very small, at its peak not more than 1 to 2 percent.

IV. Losses for the Indian textile producers were largely balanced by gains for the consumer, which were large. By 1850, prices of ordinary cloth were about 20 percent of what they were by 1800.

V.   Many of the jobs lost due to competition with mechanized textiles consisted of those held by poorly paid domestic workers with low opportunity costs.

Moreover, an alternate plausible source of economic regress in some areas was taxation, mainly because India's government of the time collected taxes more thoroughly than before in areas where direct contracts with the cultivator were in play.

Employment in agriculture: Agriculture has been the predominant sector for India's workers for the last two centuries, right up to present times. About 70 percent of India's employment was in the primary sector in the first few decades of the 20th century. The conditions for agriculture have been a primary determinant of India's economic progress and the well-being of most of its people.

"Between 1885 and 1938, cultivable area increased by 60 million acres, of which over half was irrigated. The latter half of the 19th century saw agrarian commercialization driven by trans-local markets. Early in the 19th century, India's product markets were constrained by a multiplicity of weights and measures, backward and risky transportation systems, and the extensive use of barter. But global technological advances and British administration weakened these constraints and enabled closer integration of markets. Agricultural prices consistently rose. Transactions costs fell. Land sales, land prices, and rents increased. Credit transactions expanded. Labor became more mobile and more market-oriented, and millions went overseas. Profit opportunities led to changes in resource use. For example, in what had been the drier millet zones, after irrigation, a basket of "cash crops" became common, like wheat, cotton, oilseeds, sugarcane, and tobacco. The value of India's exports quintupled between 1870 and 1914. Agricultural goods accounted for 70 to 80 percent of the exports" (Roy 2002).

Colonialism brought changes in the laborer's social position. In pre-colonial India, laborers came from castes whose primary duty was to perform labor. Many were akin to serfs, and some were actually salable. In the colonial period, this serfdom or slavery declined. The element of compulsion and force in employment weakened. The possibility of migrating to the cities and to other British colonies made occupational choices more diverse. The decline of attached labor was partly induced by the widespread exit of these castes from agricultural labor and entry into plantations, mines, urban services, public works, and government utilities.

Employment in industry: India's workforce is not significantly more industrial today than a century ago. In 1901, 13.9 million industrial workers formed 10.5 percent of the workforce. The share of industry in national income grew from 11.1 percent in the period from 1900 to 1910 to 16.4 percent between 1940 and 1946. "Factory employment in the colonial period was overwhelmingly dominated by the textile industry: mills for cotton and jute spinning and weaving; cotton-ginning firms and jute presses; and a few large firms in wool and silk spinning and weaving. The other mechanized industries were paper, sugar, matches, cement, and steel. Technology and capital goods were imported, but even significant Indian mills used a far higher proportion of labor to capital than the comparable factor proportions in the same industries in Britain. These modern factories were concentrated in two provinces, Bombay and Bengal. The attraction of these provinces, especially that of the cities of Bombay and Calcutta, derived from their position as major centers of transportation and large settlements of maritime traders" (Roy 2002).

Advent of modern industry was essentially a product of India's contact with Britain. In cotton and jute mills, the idea of a mill, the technical knowledge, the equipment and capital intensity, a part of the capital, and a section of the engineers at first came from Britain. This dependence on British precedence led to ways of organizing work that did not exist before. It gave rise to cities such as Calcutta or Bombay; shaped urban labor markets; encouraged the growth of railways, ports, laws, banks, and technical schools; and was a force behind the modernization of services (Roy 2002). Factory labor was a new form of work in India in the middle of the 19th century. Machinery, migration, urbanization, and discipline were new ingredients in the workers' lives.

Financial market: At the start of colonial rule in the 1850s, India's capital market institutions were inadequate to channel household savings to industrial investment. The real cost of capital was astronomical. The hunger of Indians for gold and silver took a toll on productive investment. The slow pace of institutional development on the financial side was also a negative factor. The traditional system normally did not deal in deposits and was thus inadequate in channeling household savings into productive uses. Such a development had to await joint stock banks, which expanded only late in the interwar period, that too in a highly unsteady fashion. It is not surprising that the pioneers in modern industry came almost entirely from communities that had specialized in trading and banking activities—that is, those who could raise money more easily. By and large, fixed capital in modern industry came from its own sources of funds or from borrowings from within a small set of people known to each other.

Increase in commercialization: Commercialization involved a number of shifts increasing integration of the market for the products of traditional manufacturing; a shift away from production for own use or use as gifts and tributes to production for the market; and a shift from local to longer distance trade. As markets integrated, competition within the crafts intensified. There was a decline of older institutional forms and the rise of new ones that used labor more efficiently. In particular, there was a decline in two types of non-specialized workers: women working in household industries and a group the early censuses called "general labor," which performed a variety of laboring tasks in the villages and some man-ufacturing on the side (Roy 2002). Leather manufacture provides an ex-ample of how commercialization affected traditional manufacturing.

Competition between traditional handloom manufacturing and the modern power loom manufacturing was acute, and the share of traditional manufacturing eroded steadily throughout the 19th century. However, hand- and power-weaving also served segmented markets, and those seg-ments of hand-weaving that did not compete with modern textile man-ufacturing saw a pattern of expansion in demand, commercialization, and urbanization, along with technological and organizational change. A range of traditional manufacturing industries intensive in craftsmanship—carpets, shawls, engraved metals, or silks—were always urban and com-mercial. But the extent of urban concentration increased, and there was a qualitative change in clientele from powerful local patrons to exports. If Bombay and Calcutta with their large-scale factories represent one face of industrialization in India, numerous medium-sized towns, such as Agra, Benares, Moradabad, Sholapur, Madurai, or Jaipur, illustrate the strength of labor-intensive industry that arose from traditional roots.

Craftsmanship was a resource contributing to industrialization in India. In the largest industry, handlooms, wages did not rise for the or-dinary weaver, but returns to capital and craftsmanship increased. This process illustrates industrialization based on utilizing labor more produc-tively, rather than on replacing labor by machinery. Commercialization started the process. There was a persistence, and even strengthening, of traditional organization in the short run. Thus, in India, both modern and traditional industry developed side by side (Roy 2002).

Movement of trade and capital: India was a more open economy in the colonial period. Before the 19th century, foreign trade was a negligible activity for India's economy as a whole, though it was significant for cer-tain regions. The ratio of trade to domestic production increased from 1 to 2 percent around 1800 to a little less than 10 percent in the 1860s to 20 percent by 1914. India's government during the colonial period bor-rowed heavily abroad to finance its investments and other commitments. Repayment of these loans, along with regular remittance on account of charges made by Britain for costs of the administration of India, was a large net payment item in India's foreign transactions. The money supply in colonial India was mainly influenced by the balance of payments. The primary objective of monetary policy was to stabilize the exchange rate. Stabilization of prices and outputs was meant to happen automatically. However, when Indian interests and Britain's interests came in conflict, stabilization in Britain's external account was usually in the minds of those who decided Indian affairs.

Critiques of colonialism emphasized payments on government account, infamous as "drain." These remittances held an element of transfer, in that some of the services for which payments were due were overpriced. The British administrative elite, for example, was paid as grandly as its counterpart in precolonial Mughal India. However, a great deal of government expenditure was made for services that India needed but could not supply on its own, such as pensions to teachers and engineers or payment of debts raised to finance railways and irrigation. After all, Britain and India were worlds apart in their technical, scientific, and managerial capabilities. "Drain," therefore, is extremely difficult to separate from legitimate factor payments (Roy 2002).

India's growth during the colonial period: The first 60 years or so of British colonialism delivered economic growth and a rising standard of living. The early colonial period between 1858 and 1914 saw positive economic growth for India. The rate of growth was small by modern standards, but not trivial by contemporary standards. India's real national income grew at over 1 percent between 1868 and 1914, and per capita income at a little less than 1 percent. These growth rates appeared to be rising late in the 19th and early 20th centuries. In contrast, the interwar period of the 1920s and 1930s was a difficult time, for the world economy, for India, for Britain, and for India–Britain relations. A combination of much slower growth in output and much more rapid growth in population meant that average the standards of living stopped improving, or even declined, and the poorer sections of the agricultural population in particular faced harder conditions.

In the 19th century, India's growth was shaped by factors tied to labor-intensive growth. Public investment—in irrigation, railways, and other public works—extended the production frontier by bringing new land under cultivation. The expansion of trade and commercialization, both between regions and internationally, took advantage of the public investments. There was also a great reallocation of labor away from settled agriculture and handicrafts to new lands and new occupations, such as plantations, mines, public works, or migration overseas. The received interpretation of colonialism tends to see this process as one of pure labor displacement. But more realistically, after the reallocations, overall labor demand increased in the 19th century.

Already by 1900, the opportunities for expanding acreage had been largely exhausted, and new land was scarce. Further growth in agriculture was based wholly on labor input. The period between 1858 and 1920 saw only a modest increase in the supply of workers. Thereafter, the growth rate of the population and the supply of labor both accelerated. In modern industry, expansion was based on growth in both capital and labor inputs. In traditional industry, there was very little growth in capital and a fall in labor input. The main source of growth was institutional changes leading to increased total factor productivity. This outcome was a result of markets and organizational change. When the products of traditional industry became more commercialized in the colonial period, two things happened. First, some low-productivity segments in handicraft textiles were destroyed by foreign competition. Secondly, and somewhat later, there was increasing competition within the domestic handicrafts. As a result, the traditional household organization tended to decay, because it was incompatible with elements of commercial production like the division of labor, economies of scale, monitoring costs, and the opportunity costs of family labor.

The mobility of labor increased as well. In India, reallocation of labor has often required more than just a wage incentive. Much of the reallocation of labor into sectors like modern industry, mines, plantations, and, to a small extent, railways, relied on "contractors," who could communicate with both the workers and the employers and who frequently took advantage of asymmetric information. After about 1900, voluntary internal migration increased, and labor became increasingly commercialized. Access to training became wider compared to that under older institutions, such as families or close-knit apprenticeship systems (Roy 2002).

Contribution of British rule: The British rule in India for about 200 years left behind some permanent imprints in the socioeconomic, political, and cultural life of Indians. India achieved political unification under the British rule. The credit for the origin of administrative machinery also goes to the British rule. The Indian Civil Service, the Indian Police Service, the Indian Audit and Account Service, the Indian Medical Service, the Indian Education Service, and the Revenue and Judicial Service created an administrative machinery that not only shouldered the responsibility of the work of the government on a large scale, but also dealt with issues such as famine and plague, means of transport and communication, agricultural projects, etc. Credit goes to the British Government for the establishment of popular educational institutions. Due to a Western education, an intellectual awakening took place among the middle-classes, who eventually led the national movement and demanded self-rule for India. However, the British government did not build an effective mass education system. Private education funding was slow. Colonial development was based on the classical principle that nations should grow by utilizing their endowments in a free world market (Roy 2002).

The Indian Renaissance and several socio-religious movements of the 19th century were the outcome of reactions against British rule and their atrocities. All these movements paved the way for the modernization of India. Many social evils were eradicated because of these movements. The British also brought in a new dimension by developing a banking system and a system of free trade. People could use now a single currency system along with the exchange rates. Weights and measures were brought into the system and trade was carried on at a large scale with the development of the railways, roads, telegraph lines, etc. However, the people of India suffered a great loss in the economic domain. Thus, the British rule in India proved both beneficial and harmful in different spheres. In fact, whatever harm the British had done to India was only to safeguard their own interests and whatever advantages the Indians received from British rule were the outcome of the efforts made by the leaders of the national movement.[2]

Endnotes

1. Economic impact of British Rule in India. https://exampariksha
.com/economic-impact-of-british-rule-in-india-history-study-
material-notes/, (accessed on December 24, 2019).
2. Contribution and Impact of British Rule on India. http://www
.historydiscussion.net/british-india/contribution-and-impact-of-
british-rule-on-india/2617, (accessed on December 24, 2019).

CHAPTER 5

Growth of the Indian Economy between 1947 and 1990

In this chapter the growth of the Indian economy since independence has been analyzed. It provides an account of India's economic development, its achievements, shortfalls, and future challenges. The economic policies and the politics behind the transformation of the Indian economy have been used as a backdrop. "India's economic journey from an impoverished country to an emerging global economy is an inspiring example for many developing nations. In order to understand India's economic voyage, it is essential to shed some light on India's political and economic history. After 200 years of British rule, India became an independent, sovereign nation in 1947. This newly born nation faced a number of issues. In 1947 when the British transferred power to India, the country inherited a crippled economy with a stagnant agriculture and a peasantry steeped in poverty" (Gosai 2013). As the first Prime Minister of India, Jawaharlal Nehru (1946) put it:

> India was under an industrial capitalist regime, but her economy was largely that of the pre-capitalist period, minus many of the wealth-producing elements of that pre-capitalist economy. She became a passive agent of modern industrial capitalism suffering all its ills and with hardly any of its advantage.

It was a mission impossible but policymakers and others of that time did their best and transformed the Indian economy. To better understand India's economic growth, its economic progress should be divided into two phases: the first 43 years after independence (up to 1990) and the next three decades (1991 to the present) as a free market economy.

During the first 43 years after independence, India promoted a mixed economic system in which the government played a major role as central planner, regulator, investor, manager, and producer. Starting in 1951, the government based its economic planning on a series of five-year plans influenced by the Soviet model. Initially, the attempt was to boost the domestic savings rate, which more than doubled in the half century following the First Five-Year Plan (1951 to 1955). With the Second Five-Year Plan (1956 to 1961), the focus began to shift to import substituting industrialization, with an emphasis on capital goods. A broad and diversified industrial base developed.

"The private sector owned and operated small- to medium-size businesses, and industries protected by the government and the government took care of everything else. The government was in charge of most of the consumer services, including transportation such as airlines, railroads, and local transportation; communication services such as postal, telephone and telegraph, and radio and television broadcasting; and social services such as education and health care. The intention of the government was to provide these services at a reasonable cost as well as employment. India adopted five-year development plans in order to improve infrastructure, agricultural production, health care, and education, but progress was extremely slow" (Gosai 2013).

Growth of agriculture and allied activities:

Agriculture and allied activities constitute the single largest contributor to the Gross Domestic Product (GDP). They, are vital to the national well-being as, besides providing the basic needs of the society and the raw materials for some of the important segments of Indian industry, they provide livelihood for almost two thirds of the work force. The share of the agricultural products in the total export earnings, both in primary and processed forms, is very significant. India's agriculture is composed of many crops, with the foremost food staples being rice and wheat. Indian farmers also grow pulses, potatoes, sugarcane, oilseeds, and such non-food items as cotton, tea, coffee, rubber, and jute (a glossy fiber used to make burlap and twine). India is a fisheries giant as well. India's production of food grains has been increasing every year, and India is among the top producers of several crops such as wheat, rice, pulses, sugarcane and cotton. It is the highest producer of milk and second highest producer of fruits and vegetables. Besides providing for the livelihood of farmers and laborers, the agricultural sector also addresses food security for the nation.[1]

Over the last 4 decades, agriculture has made important strides in the country. "Since the late 1960s the introduction of new, high-yielding hybrid varieties of seeds (HYVs), mainly for wheat and secondarily for rice, has brought about the most dramatic increases in production, especially in Punjab (where their adoption is virtually universal), Haryana, western Uttar Pradesh, and Gujarat. So great has been the success of the so-called Green Revolution that India was able to build up buffer stocks of grain sufficient for the country to weather several years of disastrously bad monsoons with virtually no imports or starvation and even to become, in some years, a modest net food exporter" (Encyclopaedia Britannica). It has been able to meet the growing demand of the increasing population for their essential consumption. At the same time, it is necessary to ensure that the process of development is sustainable. Despite the overwhelming size of the agricultural sector, however, yields per hectare of crops in India are generally low compared to international standards and agricultural growth has been fairly volatile.

Key issues affecting agricultural productivity include the decreasing sizes of agricultural land holdings, continued dependence on the monsoon, inadequate access to irrigation, imbalanced use of soil nutrients resulting in loss of fertility of soil, uneven access to modern technology in different parts of the country, lack of access to formal agricultural credit, limited procurement of food grains by government agencies, and failure to provide remunerative prices to farmers.[2] These problems have continued to frustrate India for decades. It is estimated that as much as one-fifth of the total agricultural output is lost due to inefficiencies in harvesting, transport, and storage of government-subsidized crops.[3]

Livestock: Animal husbandry is one of the important sub sector of agricultural economy and plays a significant role in the rural economy by providing gainful employment particularly to the small/marginal farmers, women and agricultural landless laborers. This sector also provides milk, eggs, meat, wool, hides and skin, dung, bones, hooves and draught power. Manures and slaughter house by-products are also sources of energy. "The contribution of the livestock sector has increased to about Rs. 27,700 crores in 1987–88 as compared to Rs. 10,600 crores in 1980–81 which constitutes 25.5 per cent of the total agricultural output. The animal husbandry sector has made good progress in the livestock production and health" (Planning Commission, Eighth Plan, Vol. 2).

Forestry: The total forest cover is 708,273 square km, which is 21.54 percent of the total area of the country.[4] Forests play an important role in the India's socio-economic development. They are rich sources of energy, housing, firewood, timber and fodder and they provide employment to a large section of the rural population. Demand for forest products and services in the country is increasing with economic growth, industrialization and increase in population. A large section of population depends upon forests for their livelihood. Commercial forestry is not highly developed in the country.

Fisheries: The major constraints in fisheries were over-concentration on shrimp fishing, non-exploitation of unconventional fishery resources in the marine sector and slow progress in the expansion of extensive and semi-intensive aquaculture systems in the inland and brackish-water fisheries. Processing and marketing facilities for sea food and inland fish were inadequate. The Fishery Survey of India carried out studies on assessment of suitable craft and gears for marine fisheries and disseminated information about fishery resources availability. In the inland water fisheries sector, the establishment of about 300 Fish Farmers Development Agencies (FFDA) and fish seed production by circular Chinese type of hatcheries etc. contributed to an increase in the average yield (Planning Commission, Eighth Plan, Vol. 2).

Industrial development:
The industrial sector was to play a key role in the achievement of such socio-economic change and public enterprise was seen as harbinger of

this transformation. This gave rise to the concept of a mixed economy in so far as industry sector was concerned, with primacy of emphasis on the role of the state in the development for the modern industries base. State control and ownership of industries reflected the economic thinking and ethos of the times and was "the best that could have been expected, given the domestic and world environment extant at the time" (Rakesh Mohan 1992).

The Industrial Policy Resolution of April 1948 was the first document to provide insights on how the industrial structure was to evolve over a period to time. The Second Resolution of 1956 was a reflection of the economic diversification envisaged as part of the strategy of development. P C Mahalanobis (1961, 1963) was the architect of the strategy.

As a corollary to the industrialization strategy, and in support of it, the industrial licensing mechanism was evolved and strengthened over time till the early seventies. The fundamental basis for industrial licensing was provided by the Industries (Development and Regulation) Act (IDRA), 1951. Form the early fifties and eighties industrial licensing and a series of control in the sphere of industrial activities had created distortions in allocative efficiency, and constricted domestic production and competitiveness in the Indian industry. Industrial licensing was gradually relaxed since the mid-seventies and more sharply since the mid-eighties with favorable effects on industrial production.

The government exercised other controls such as on raising of capital issues, prices and production of selected commodities, foreign exchanges, export import allocation of credit etc., as part of the development strategy.

The experience of the eighties showed that industrial growth could pick up if barriers to entry were eliminated and units were given freedom to produce products that markets demanded. It had also become clear that public sector could not expand and needed to improve its competitive positions. The pick-up in capital market activity showed that industrial financing could be increasingly undertaken from private funds. The experience also revealed that if Indian industrial units were to be rendered competitive, they could gain higher shares in the international markets, besides improving the availability of industrial goods in the domestic markets (Sharma 1997).

Banking and finance:

India's financial system, as of now, is large with a variety of banks, financial institutions, capital market institutions, non-banks and a number of indigenous banking and financial institutions, going beyond the dichotomy prevalent in the pre-independence period of organized and unorganized financial sectors.

The prime focus of the development of Indian banking system has basically been confined to ensure timely and adequate credit support for the viable and productive sectors of the economy. Indeed, nationalization of major banks in 1969 was a historic step in recognition of the potential of the banking system to promote broader economic objectives viz. growth, regional balance and diffusion of economic power. Since nationalization, Indian banking industry has made an impressive progress, especially in extending geographical spread and functional reach. There has been a considerable change in the structure and progress of banks during the pre-as well as post-bank nationalization period.

Since independence "the Indian capital market has evolved into a dynamic system of the Indian financial system. The primary capital market has developed as an important source of funding aided by amiable public policies, product innovation, and institutionalization. Improvement in infrastructure, adoption of state-of-art technologies and streamlining of the regulatory framework have up graded the Indian stock market to the international standards" (Misra 1997).

External sector:

Policy makers in independent India supported the external sector by a combination of initial increase in import, adaptation, protection and cautious utilization of scarce foreign exchange resources. Import substitution was accepted as not only a 'correct strategy but also inevitable in a continental economy such as India'. Even as export-pessimism coupled with import substitution continued to hold sway, a realization that exports could still be promoted through concerted government action was also gaining ground. "The crafting of the change in the policy stance was fashioned by the recommendations of a number of committees which were set up during the seventies and eighties" (Kapur 1997). Foreign investment policy during the late sixties and seventies was marked by tight regulation and discretionary control. Towards the end of the eighties alongside the growing importance of external transactions in economic activity, there have been fundamental shifts in the policy approach.

Social sector and poverty: The Indian state has been more penetrated by social actors. Alleviation of poverty has been one of the main objectives since the beginning of the plan periods. However, the combined effect of growth through trickle down and direct attack through various anti-poverty programmes has been quite dismal. Even though poverty ratio has witnessed some decline in the eighties and nineties, the level has remained high. Deaton and Dreze (2007) point out that the number of Indians living at less than a dollar a day has come down, even though there is a substantial debate about the extent of decline in the poverty rate. "The lack of effective targeting of public distribution system (PDS), backtracking from land reform measures, inadequate attention to primary education and health care system have been the missing links" (Mohapatra 1997). India's public health record presents a dismal picture. The infant mortality rate declined by 30 percent in the 1980s. India's growth has produced more development for the rich and the middle class than the poorest sections of society. India's growth has increased economic inequality.

"The trajectory of economic policies favoring India's growth was path dependent. From 1947 to 1975 the policy consensus favored an important role of the state within a relatively closed economy. Private enterprise survived during this period but India's trade declined. Changes in the policy consensus favoring economic deregulation began to appear in the mid-1970s, which prepared the ground for the tectonic policy shifts beyond 1991. The major challenge for India's development is inclusive growth. Growth has unambiguously reduced poverty and improved the human condition in India. But the gains of the middle and richer classes have been greater than those that went to the poorer sections of society" (Mukherji 2009).

India's Growth Trajectory since Independence

From 1950 to 1980, India's real GDP grew at an annual average rate of 3.6 percent (1.5 percent in per capita terms). The shift to a higher growth path during the course of the 1980s is referred to as the Indian growth turnaround. Fast growth in India since the early 1980s has placed it among the top nine rapidly growing economies in the world (Ahmed and Varshney 2009). An analysis of aggregate data suggests a pickup in growth during the early 1980s, before most of the major policy changes. The low growth in the first phase is referred to as the "Hindu rate of growth," a period in which import duties were among the highest in the world, foreign direct investment (FDI) was prohibited in many sectors of the economy, and there was extensive regulation of interest rates. The upward shift in India's growth path during the 1980s is significant for two reasons: The turnaround happened well before the balance of payments (BoP) crisis of 1991 and the large-scale macroeconomic reforms that ensued.

"It was the service sector that led the increase in the overall growth rate in the early 1980s. Since many components of services are income related (such as financial services, business services, and hotels and restaurants) and begin to increase only after a certain stage in development, the fact that India's service sector created the impulse for the growth turnaround is puzzling. What is indisputable is that something happened during the 1980s that opened the door to a rise in growth" (Ghate and Wright 2010).

It is commonly believed India's growth acceleration was mainly due to a change in the state's attitude toward the business sector from being antibusiness to being probusiness in the early 1980s and less to do with changes in economic policies. Sen (2007) finds little empirical support, however, for the argument that the state's attitudinal shift to the private sector in the 1980s was the primary cause of India's growth acceleration. He has argued that the effect of the attitudinal shift of the state toward the private sector on India's growth acceleration was second order, and if it did have an effect on growth at all, it was only through changes in economic policies, rather than independently of the latter. He favors a "back to basics" story of India's growth acceleration. The increase in economic growth occurred due to three policy-influenced fundamentals:

A) Financial deepening
B) A rise in public investment
C) A fall in the relative price of equipment

From the "mid-1970s to the early 1980s, financial deepening, which was a consequence of the bank nationalization of 1969, and an increase in public fixed investment were the key factors for India's growth acceleration. Growth was sustained from the early 1980s onward by the fall in the relative price of equipment investment brought about by trade reforms targeting the capital and intermediate goods sectors. Thus, India's growth acceleration can be attributed in its early phase to a classically statist model of development and in its later phase to economic reforms that significantly altered the rules of the game with respect to the integration of Indian firms with the world economy" (Sen 2007). India is today a changed country from what it was half a century ago. It still has huge challenges staring it in the face, but at the same time, the country has long since broken with the "Hindu rate of growth"; its population below the poverty line has fallen steadily since the late 1960s, and sharply over the last decade; and it has joined the pantheon of major players globally.

It seems quite remarkable that India did what no other newly independent developing country did. It invested in politics first—establishing democracy, free speech, independent media, and equal rights for all citizens. While a large part of the credit for this does go to the early political leaders, such as Mahatma Gandhi, Nehru, and Ambedkar, and to progressive writers and intellectuals, such as Rabindranath Tagore, Periyar E.V. Ramasamy, and Sarojini Naidu, as in all matters of history, luck also plays a role. And India had it in ample measure. In any case, the upshot was that in terms of political design and structure, with regular elections, a progressive constitution, secularism, free media, and an empowered supreme court, India resembled an advanced nation, and in this respect had very few peers in the developing world (Basu 2018).

India's downside turned out to be its economy. With growth sluggish, large swathes of population living in abject poverty, and widespread illiteracy, the country trudged along decade after decade. Despite overall growth remaining subdued at around 3.5 percent per annum, much was happening beneath that. India tried to institute five-year planning, with an effort to set up heavy industries, large-scale steel production, and dam building to generate electricity on a large scale. Somewhere in the mid-1960s India had a successful green revolution and broke out of the trap of low agricultural productivity and frequent famines. Though this was most visible in Punjab, Haryana, and western Uttar Pradesh, its benefits were felt across the nation.

Sivasubronian's (2000) comprehensive statistical study shows that annual growth, from being negligible during the first 50 years of the 20th century, moved up to somewhere between 3 and 3.5 percent in the decades immediately after the country's independence in 1947. Nayyar (2006) in his Kingsley Martin lecture at Cambridge University, in fact, identifies 1951 and 1980 as the two turning points in India's growth in the 20th century. Growth declined between 1979 and 1980; it had plummeted to 5.2 percent, the worst year in India's history from 1947 to now. In fact, after 1979 to 1980, India has not had a single year of negative GDP growth.

"What India meant by the term "socialism" (and pursued—that too without much success) was a kind of welfare state, in which there would be support for the poor in terms of health care, education, and basic food. But even this was more often present in writings emerging from the government than in actual action. In terms of the government owning the means of production, India was nowhere near a socialist state: India had roughly 14 percent of the GDP coming from state-owned enterprises, whereas for China this was 40 percent. These data are not easy to compute, and there is indeed a big margin for error, but the large difference is significant"(Basu 2018).

Democracy is a remarkable achievement for India. It needs to be appreciated that this, like good infrastructure, is an institutional and political investment that modern India has inherited and it would be folly to damage it just when the nation has reached a stage where it is able to take advantage of and build on it to power its economy, promote development, and even step up the GDP growth rate.

Good growth is the outcome of various factors: the nature of institutions in the nation, the prevalent social norms, the positioning of the nation in the global polity, and the nature of the economic policy pursued by the government. Some of the drivers of growth are beyond the control of any individual or organization. But there are also some that can be shaped by the government and individuals in the nation. Economic growth does not occur solely because of good economics, but is due to many other factors that lie beyond mainstream economics (Basu 2018).

Barring the growth spike in 1975, the nation chugged along at a fairly steady low-growth rate, of around 3.5 percent per annum, for the first three decades. Given that India's population was initially growing at over 2 percent per annum, this meant a snail's pace growth of barely over 1 percent for per capita income. Table 5.1 presents the annual GDP growth rate, averaged over decades, and shows India growing at 3.91 percent, 3.68 percent, and 3.09 percent over the 1950s, 1960s, and 1970s, respectively. In decadal terms, the big break was in the 1980s, when the growth breached the 5 percent mark for the first time.

Table 5.1 India's decadal GDP growth and investment rates

Year	Annual GDP growth rate	Investment rate	Savings rate
1951–1961	3.91	11.82	–
1961–1971	3.68	14.71	9.03
1971–1981	3.09	17.86	12.96
1981–1991	5.38	21.04	17.32
1991–2001	5.71	24.14	24.27
2001–2011	7.68	32.44	31.42
2011–2018	6.61	35.78	31.17

Notes: The GDP growth rate before 2011 is shown at factor cost, at constant prices, with 2004–2005 as base; the GDP growth rate after 2011 is shown at factor cost, at constant prices, with 2011–2012 as base; and Investment rate refers to gross capital formation as a percentage of GDP. *Source:* Economic Survey 2017–2018, Government of India, 2018.

Growth picked up through the 1980s owing to freed up markets and eased controls, which were beginning to smother the country's growth. But, by the end of the 1980s, more than anything else, it was fiscal laxity that helped India grow faster and also set the stage for the big crisis of 1990 to 1991, when the first Gulf War precipitated a massive slowdown and a BoP crisis for India (Basu 2018). The broad direction of India's growth is upward; there is indeed a sharp rise in growth between the 1970s and 1980s. There were some important policy drivers behind the growth pickup, including greater reliance on markets and less on the state. From the mid-1980s fiscal fueling contributed to the growth but also to the economic crisis of 1990 to 1991.

Turning to economic policy, the most important story was that of savings and investment. What arguably gave a boost to savings, and therefore, investment was the decision to nationalize all banks in 1969. One consequence of this was that there was a sudden rise in the number of bank branches in relatively remote rural areas (a consequence of a directive from the government to the state-owned banks). This made it easier for people to save money, and through the 1970s there was a steep and unprecedented rise in India's savings rate. The *spread of banking facilities* in India played a positive role in promoting savings. Public savings tend to boost overall savings because, although public savings displace private savings, this displacement effect is muted.

India saw a most unusual growth pattern for a developing country. It was not the manufacturing sector that led India's growth but the services sector. Over the next 15 years India services sector growth was primarily because of the information technology sector, in which the country excelled. To complete the picture of how India has developed overall, it is important to look at other primary indicators of progress: literacy, poverty, inequality, and health. The story here has been less encouraging. For a nation committed to equality and socialism, India did surprisingly poorly on these important indicators of overall development (Basu 2018). Poverty has been declining, but with over 20 percent of the population living on less than $1.90 a day and 60 percent living on $3.20 a day or less, there is still a great distance to go. These indicators provide little comfort and the nation cannot be unmindful of the fact that they can become a drag on overall development and even GDP growth. "Inequality numbers are dismaying as socialism in India is mainly a rhetorical exercise". In a nation that now has several individuals listed among the world's wealthiest individuals, the numbers on poverty tell us that India does have work to do in reversing some of these inequality trends.

To conclude, the country's development indicators have changed in the last half century. The country has experienced an increase in per capita income—especially since the 1980s—as well as reductions in poverty and infant mortality rates. These improvements are not insignificant and mark a sharp break from the near stagnation that the country experienced during British rule. For several hundred million poor people in delicate health and with little education, however, the country will have to find a way to overcome the technical, institutional, and economic barriers to developing the capabilities necessary for functioning of the economy.

Endnotes

1. State of Agriculture in India. http://prsindia.org/policy/discussion-papers/state-agriculture-india, (accessed on December 25, 2019).
2. Ibid.
3. India – Agriculture. https://www.nationsencyclopedia.com/economies/Asia-and-the-Pacific/India-AGRICULTURE.html,   (accessed   on December 25, 2019).
4. Ghosh, S. February 16, 2018. State of Forest Report says that India's forest and tree cover has increased by 1 percent. https://india.mongabay.com/2018/02/state-of-forest-report-says-that-indias-forest-and-tree-cover-has-increased-by-1-percent/, (accessed on December 25, 2019).

CHAPTER 6

Policy Framework: State and Market

The focus of this chapter is to analyze the role of government in regulating the various sectors of the economy and its response to market failures. Institutions as central to the economy as government, business, and law have been reformed from generation to generation, and an awareness of past changes in these institutions is needed to appreciate the significance of present day events.

Whatever one may think of a market-driven economy, no one would want a completely market-driven society; hence, the universal agreement on the need for laws, rules, and institutions to *govern* the functioning of markets and of individual and corporate behavior. What these look like is, of course, the very stuff of politics, as well as of moral philosophy. According to Nobel Laureate W Arthur Lewis (1955)

No country has made economic progress without *positive stimulus from intelligent government.* On the other hand, there are so many examples of the mischief done to economic life by governments that it is easy to fill one's pages with warnings against government participation in economic life.

Sensible people do not get involved in arguments about whether economic progress is due to government activity or to individual initiative; they know that it is due to both, and they concern themselves only with asking *what is the proper contribution of each.* (Hudson 2015)

Governments may fail because they either do too little or do too much.
Cairncross (1966) has observed that

> government intervention has *developed piecemeal*, each measure
> being adopted on its merits and only rarely in order to give effect
> to some theory of economic organization. No one can claim to
> have foreseen, much less planned, the present blend of private
> enterprise and public control, although a mixed economy of some
> sort has long been recognized as desirable and indeed inevitable. A
> theory of controls is correspondingly difficult to construct except
> as a critique of the controls that are in being at some point in time.

Even in capitalist countries there are certain aspects where government intervention is required for better performance of the economy. A certain consensus seems to be emerging these days on the role the government is supposed to play on the economic front.

Market failure: Even though markets may be the best way of organizing production and distributing goods and services, there are important instances when they fail to produce efficient outcomes. This is because market forces (Asher 1994)

    I. do not bring in competition in its fullest sense;

   II. often lead to the creation of monopolies and oligopolies;

  III. divert investment to those directions in which profits are high, neglecting low-profit but high-utility socially necessary production;

  IV. lead to increasing disparities in income and wealth;

   V. do not ensure that prosperity at the top will trickle down to the bottom;

  VI. fail in macroeconomic coordination;

 VII. fail to control monopoly power;

VIII. problem of public goods and externalities; and

  IX. existence of asymmetric information.

Besides the aforementioned types of market failure, reservations about the efficiency of capital and insurance markets, and concern for values other than efficiency, such as equity; including income; consumption;

distribution; freedom; and human dignity; provide the analytical rationale for the role of government in a modern economy. There is no market force model that can show in a valid manner that it can make the poorest groups attain within a reasonable period an acceptable standard of life.

The debate on the respective roles of state and market continues unabated. The two extreme poles of views are the advocacy on the one hand of *state minimalism* and on the other of *pervasive government intervention* to foster rapid economic development.

The disputes relate mostly to the objectives and modalities of governmental interventions in these processes. In the 1960s, the transaction cost approach of *Coase (1960)* argued in favor of a superior authority that is essential for fair play in the market. The case for effective state intervention can also be found in the social choice theories of *Sen (2008) and others like Arrow (1951)*. The effectiveness of the state or the market in economic intervention cannot be argued in a vacuum. Much depends on the nature of the state and the structure of markets.

It has also been argued that government intervention becomes more relevant in the provision of *public goods* that are *nonrival* and *nonexcludable*. *Market failure* can be corrected in a number of ways. In situations where markets do not perform their functions properly, the first task of the government must be to make the market work efficiently by appropriate institutional and legal changes. The 1950s were probably the heydays of government intervention. The interventionist state in many countries resulted in economic losses not only due to misallocation of resources arising from faulty investment decisions but also due to diversion of resources to *rent-seeking* activities because of the very regulations themselves. Analysts began to describe the situation as one of "government failure."

Government failure: While the state took a lead in initiating the process of development, the adverse consequences of the process were many. *The government machinery and bureaucratic apparatus went on expanding. The state stretched its arms even to areas where it was not necessary. The state took too much upon itself in the name of development.* In the course of time, people came to depend upon the state for everything and lost their initiative. A top–down approach, insensitivity to differentiated needs at the local level, inefficient implementation, wastage and leakage in developmental spending are all very familiar consequences. The expansion in economic activities led, in due course, to intensive examination of the concept of government failure. Asher (1994) has provided the following reasons for such failures:

I. The consequences of many government actions are extremely complicated and difficult to foresee.

II. Government may promulgate policy measures, but it has only a limited control over relevant variables.

III. There is a gap between legislation and intention, and between those who set a broad policy framework on the one hand and those who frame detailed rules and procedures and who actually implement them on a day to day basis on the other.

IV. Different interest groups may vie with each other in a society, and this may complicate the task of defining what is overall public interest.

V. Due to regulatory capture, regulation may be serving the interest of the regulated; no incentive towards efficiency.

VI. *The Dagli Committee on controls and subsidies* (May 1979) pointed out several instances where controls had lost rationale or were working unsatisfactorily.

Emerging consensus on the changed role of government: A certain consensus seems to have emerged on the role the government is supposed to play on the economic front. As regards the modus operandi of government intervention, the tendency is to adopt measures operating through the market mechanism in preference to command and control measures. The issue today is no longer "rivalry" between the state and the market but how to achieve "synergy." The assumption that the state has no role in economic activity and markets do not fail has proved to be incorrect. Several public sector enterprises (PSEs) continue to run efficiently in India. Both PSEs and private enterprises could achieve "efficiency" and "welfare" (United Nations 2008).

"In order to attack "market failures" public enterprises must avoid "government failures" as well as consequent "managerial failure" in their operation. Managerial failure invariably follows from the inability of governments to adopt sound policies on investment, prices, and financing as well as on new projects and several other areas affecting the management of PSEs. Inability of governments to build managerial cadres for PSEs and provide the managerial cadres with necessary autonomy to run PSEs with efficiency and welfare can also result in managerial failures" (Basu 2005). There is need for laying down clear guidelines on selective privatization as well as for institutionalizing the "partnership" between the government and PSEs without diluting the government's accountability.

Rangarajan (2000) has rightly observed that

> the decreasing role of the State as a producer of goods and services and the increasing role of the market in such areas simultaneously enhance the role of the State as a *'regulator'*. *Tony Blair and Gerhard Schroder* summed up the position by remarking, *'The State should not row but steer'*. The regulatory role of the Government in the financial and other sectors has assumed added importance in the context of the East Asian and other crises. The regulatory role also comes into play in order to maintain competitive conditions in the market. The 'facilitator' role relates to the provision of public goods. However, even here there is a changing perception. It is no longer necessary for the state to participate directly in the investment in physical infrastructure. Private investment under a suitable regulatory and tariff authority may yet fill the need, even though the role of direct investment by the State in the emerging economies in these areas will be dominant for quite some time. But in the area of social infrastructure such as health and education, the direct participatory role of the State is clearly seen. That is why the paradoxical statement *'More market does not mean less government but different government'*.

Given the respective roles of state and market in the economy, it goes without saying that in areas where direct state intervention is necessary, it is important to ensure that the state functions efficiently and fulfills the stated objectives.

According to Rangarajan (2000)

the major question of determining how much of state intervention still remains. One test for determining the respective roles of state and market is the application of the principle of comparative advantage. Given a particular objective, it may be possible to examine *the comparative advantage of State intervention versus market intervention in achieving the objective.* Within State intervention, it may be necessary to examine whether ownership by government or regulation is the most effective method for achieving the desired objective. In some activities, separating funding from providing the service can be attempted and the advantage of combining government and market in different proportions can be explored.

"One must make the point that the market and state intervention must go together in the interests of development with equity. There is neither magic in the marketplace nor divinity in the invisible hand of the market. Instead of jumping to oversimplified conclusions, it is essential to recognize that markets can only service those who are part of the market system. In rural India, about 300 million people who take out a bare subsistence, or live in absolute poverty, are not even remotely integrated with markets. For an economy at India's levels of income and development, there is a vital role for the government, although there is a clear need for change in the nature of the intervention. The market is a good servant but a bad master. One would do well to remember the wisdom, lest there be confusion between means and ends" (Singh 1999).

Changing role of government in India: India has a mixed economy that is increasingly accepting the fact that government has to play an important role in the economy. The government has invariably felt at varying degree of intensity the need for a public policy that could direct, promote or control, or regulate business activities in accordance with the goals and objectives of the economy. Thus, public sector and private sector do exist with varying degrees of importance in the economy.

Planned approach meant that the State should take initiative in creating facilities and institutions that contribute to development. Necessary resources have to be obtained through taxation, through borrowing and, if necessary, through printing money for financing the development. Mixed Economy was acceptable to many but unidirectional in role of state approach was not. The approach to efficiency was to nationalize, expand public enterprise and centralize, and no attention was paid to outcome. From 1978 onwards, balance shifted somewhat in favor of private sector. It was good to be a planner, but some doubted (Reddy 2017b). World was changing, but India did not change much in terms of policies. There was some rethinking, however, about the controls. A number of reports by government committees were submitted to rebalancing the role of the state and the government and the private sector. In such a framework, goods in which the "price mechanism" is effective ("low public good characteristics") need not be paid for by the government; however, the approach toward them would need to be calibrated depending on the levels of "market failure." Where market failures abound, the government will need to take a more active approach in directing the provision of the goods with, where necessary, even using taxation-like tools to compel "poorly behaved" consumes to pay for the service. Where market failures are not very glaring in that case emphasis should be on mild regulation and ensuring competitive markets would be all that is necessary to produce welfare maximization. In the areas where the price mechanism is ineffective and measurability is low, as in the case of primary education, the government would need to both pay and provide, taking great care to address the challenges associated with provision by the public sector. Only when the need arises, however, would the public sector slowly expand into other areas.

Curative health care, despite being a "private good," suffers from very high levels of market failure, and the government must intervene aggressively to direct the evolution of the health system. "Repealing obsolete laws is both obvious and relatively easy, and will free up some state capacity. The government has taken small steps in this direction. But the bigger gains will come from structural reform to streamline the regulatory process. Labor regulation is a particularly messy and entangled regulatory system. There is an opportunity to reduce the burden on the state by streamlining the current labor law system. Service law and tax codes are also obvious areas for reform. A rupee saved is a rupee earned, and state capacity freed is state capacity built" (Rajagopalan 2017). A classic example of overregulation was the license raj in India. In the 1980s, India began to reform its economy, adopting more probusiness policies.

In the Indian context, "market will not succeed unless they are supported by adequate governance institutions. Dixit (2004) has very succinctly analyzed the issue of state and market. He has observed that "most economic activities and interactions share several properties that together create the demand for an institutional infrastructure of governance. Conventional economic theory recognizes the importance of law for governance, but it takes the existence of a well-functioning law and legal system for granted. It assumes that the state has a monopoly over the use of coercion. It also assumes that the state designs and enforces laws with the objective of maximizing social welfare." The usual implicit assumption is that the law operates in a costless manner. About 40 years ago, economists realized that these assumptions are not valid since there are transactions costs, information asymmetries, principal–agent problems, and incentives.

"In the economist's ideal picture, the government supplies legal institutions that are guided solely by concern for social welfare, and such institutions operate at low cost, in the sense, they are too small to matter. In reality, the apparatus of law could be costly, slow, weak, and even biased. What happens if transaction costs are high and the legal system too slow or weak? Economic activity does not grind to a halt because the government cannot or does not provide an adequate underpinning of law" (Dixit 2004). "For many people, too much potential value would go unrealized. Individuals, groups, and societies, therefore, create alternative institutions, instruments, and practices to provide the necessary economic governance. For instance, it is widely recognized that it is difficult to have smooth business transactions without recourse to use of black money either directly or indirectly (say through input suppliers or liaison officers). It is easier to grow from a low level of income per head to a middle level than it is to remain a middle-income country and reach a high level. In the first phase of the growth or transition, economic activity is on a small scale, trade is localized, and economic transactions involve a relatively small group of people" (Reddy 2017b).

"In such a setting, networks of information flows, norms of behavior, and sanctions for deviants may already be present from the social environment, or can develop quickly as people interact economically among themselves. Self-enforcing governance is, therefore, feasible" (Dixit 2004). But for sustained growth, rule-based governance must prevail over relation-based ones. Relation-based and rule-based systems are conceptually pure categories that mix in different ways in practice. In some situations, the diminishing returns of a relation-based system can be countered without going to a fully centralized rule-based alternative. The processes of creating the institutions and the apparatus of state law, and of improving them to the point where rule-based governance dominates and functions well, can be slow and costly. The fixed costs of rule-based governance are a public investment; therefore, society must solve a collective action problem to put such a system in place (Dixit 2004).

"This is not automatic; there are the usual problems of free riding, underestimation of the benefits to future generations in today's political process, and the veto power held by those who stand to lose from the change" (Dixit 2004). Even when the public investment for a rule-based system has been made, people used to the relation-based system who want to switch must make some private investments to learn the rules and their operation. Their benefit from the switch will depend on how many others make the switch. This positive feedback externality can lead to too few switchers, or even a lock-in that keeps the old system in use. In turn, the expectation of this can reduce the social benefits of the changeover, and therefore, delay or deter the initial public investment. The benefits of the new system may be unequally distributed, and some participants may even lose. The system of rules and their enforcement itself must at first establish a reputation for integrity and efficacy. This takes a long time and strict supervision even given much goodwill (Dixit 2004). There are inherent challenges in moving from relation-based systems to rule-based systems. In dealing with this issue, one cannot take a simplistic view of a benevolent state versus a malevolent market participant. It is interesting that people urge severe actions by government where government is reputed to be weak in governance systems. Reddy (2017b) has raised a very relevant question: If corruption is a consequence of weak governance, how could empowering precisely the same governance systems solve the problem on a firm footing?

Rebalancing the role of the State: Given the change in the state of the Indian economy, there is a need to rebalance the respective roles of the state and the market on the following lines (Reddy 2017b):

    I. Reinterpretation of what constitutes public goods
   II. Using of private sector for providing public goods through competitive mechanisms, but funding by government
  III. Merit goods can have a combination of funding and provision by public and private sector
  IV. Technology makes it difficult to get a "fix" on the product, its use, and so on; hence, "control"
   V. What constitutes a monopoly has been redefined, unbundling all natural monopolies
  VI. Assessing relative efficiency of regulated private monopoly and state-owned monopoly
 VII. With regard to externalities, whether externalities have been overstated, whether they can be measured, and if they cannot be measured, how can bureaucrats administer externalities

Two Is—Ideology and Investments—were driving the relative roles of state and market in the 1950s and 1960s, but the scenario is different now. The two Is will be replaced by the five Is (Reddy 2017b):

    I. Interests
   II. Incentives
  III. Information
  IV. Innovations
   V. Institutions

The debate over state versus market has resurfaced and is being discussed vigorously in the context of the economic reforms being implemented in India. All governments have an urge to control, an urge to regulate, an urge to become overbearing. That is inconsistent with the post-reforms mind-set where governments had to become facilitators. The government's urge to control has to be restrained.[1] The idea that the state or the government can make up for failure of the market is not entirely correct. The state also has failures. So, it is necessary to weigh the strengths and weaknesses of state and market, and then define the boundaries of the state on that basis (Reddy 2017b).

Endnote

1. The Statesman. July 24, 2016. "Govt Must Resist Urge to Control Everything, Says Arun Jaitley." https://www.thestatesman.com/india/govt-must-resist-urge-to-control-everything-says-arun-jaitley-156059.html

CHAPTER 7

NITI Aayog: A Think Tank

There were wide-ranging discussions on the role and remit of the new institution to replace the Planning Commission ever since Shri Narendra Modi, the prime minister in his 2014 Independence Day address declared that the Planning Commission would be replaced by a new institution. In line with the government of India's approach of less government and a move away from centralized planning, the NITI (National Institution for Transforming India) Aayog with a new structure and focus on policy formally replaced the 64-year-old Planning Commission, in January 2015, the brainchild of Pandit Jawaharlal Nehru that was seen as a vestige of the socialist era.

> Nevertheless, while the working of the earlier plan body showed up shortcomings from time to time, it did sterling work from the ground up. It mapped the resources available in the country and pointed to the need of developing the physical and the social infrastructure in an extremely poor society by sending resources in directions in which they were needed (Dab 2016).

The replacement of the Planning Commission with a new institution, more relevant and responsive to the present economic needs and climate in the country, had long been demanded and expected. This was not the first time a government had been dismissive of the commission. Rajiv Gandhi had called the commission "a bunch of jokers." But he stopped short of dismantling it. Former Planning Commission deputy chairmen like K.C. Pant and even Manmohan Singh made some attempts to explore changes. In 2009, Dr. Singh alluded to the Planning Commission having outlived its utility and asked the members to consider changes to make it more relevant. In 2010, Arun Maira, a member of the Planning Commission, recommended changes in its structure, role, functions, and resources. Maira reveals that in 2012, a Parliamentary Standing Committee also gave a report that said that it was time for an independent evaluation of the functioning of the Planning Commission. From a highly centralized planning system, the Indian economy was gradually moving toward indicative planning, where the commission's role was changing gradually.

Rationale for NITI Aayog: In Sanskrit, *NITI* can mean *morality, behavior, guidance, politics, management, and a dozen other things*. But, in the present context, it means policy. On August 13, 2014, the union cabinet approved the repeal of the cabinet resolution dated March 15, 1950, by which the Planning Commission was set up. In countries such as the United States think tanks that function independently of the government have a major role in policymaking. In India, too, there is a great deal of economic activity that happens outside the government setup, and there is a need to design policies for such public sector entities as well.

The government plans to adopt a new approach to development. India needs an administration paradigm in which the *government is an enabler rather than a provider* of first and last resort. The institutions of governance and policy have to adapt to new challenges and must be built on the founding principles of the constitution. There is a need to separate the planning process from the strategy of governance. Transforming India will involve changes of *two* types—*consequences of market forces and those that would be planned*. The intent is made amply clear: old-style central planning is out, new-style reforms agenda is in.

The maturing of the institutions and polity also entails a diminished role for centralized planning, which itself needs to be redefined. A state-of-the-art resource center for good governance practices is also proposed. NITI Aayog bids farewell to a *one-size-fits-all* approach toward development. It emphasizes India's diversity and plurality. The Aayog would foster a spirit of "cooperative federalism" with the sole principle of developing a pro-people, proactive, and participative development agenda stressing on empowerment and equality. NITI Aayog would be the "policy commission" for India to achieve its economic potential. The name NITI

Aayog has both institution and commission in it. While Aayog stands for *commission*, one of the "Is" in NITI is for *institution*. The penchant for catchy abbreviations seems to have overlooked the oddity. Now, either it is a commission or an institution. Both terms can be interchangeable, but in that case, one of them would be redundant.[1]

According to the cabinet resolution, the rationale for setting up the Aayog were as follows:

   I. The centralized planning concept cannot work in the changed circumstances as the commission is losing its relevance. Times have changed and issues have changed and *Nehru* himself would have been the first to say that the commission needs a relook had he been alive. When private investment far exceeds public investment resulting in considerable change in center–state relations. In a market economy, the planning process needs a different orientation and outlook. This is, of course, another way of saying that it is the market that will determine priorities and the allocation of resources to various sectors, and not any planning authority.

  II. The commission has become an agent of the ruling political party or coalition at the center.

 III. The Planning Commission did very little to plan and implement even public sector investments for infrastructure, and its role in promoting public–private partnership was mostly seen as obstructive.

 IV. In the changed scenario, the states want more say in a federal setup. It is impossible for the nation to develop unless the states develop. The process of policy planning also has to change from "top to bottom" to "bottom to top." The new body will adopt a 'bottom up" approach, where decisions will be taken at the local level and then endorsed at the central level. The new body is envisaged to follow the norm of "cooperative federalism," giving room to states to tailor schemes to suit their unique needs rather than be dictated to by the center. This is meant to be a recognition of the country's diversity.

  V. States would have a key role in the new body with an effective mechanism to address interstate disputes. NITI Aayog aims to foster cooperative federalism through structured support initiatives and mechanisms with the states on a continuous basis, recognizing that strong states make a strong nation. It promises to promote the spirit of federalism in both planning and the center's disbursal of funds to the states.

VI. The role of the Planning Commission after liberalization had nothing to do with keeping the commanding heights of the economy with the public sector. The public sector itself needs reforms. Alagh (2014) feels that the Planning Commission could be replaced by a more focused body concentrating on issues like energy, water, and demographics. These issues have long-term perspectives. The NITI Aayog will be better placed to be an adviser. And it should not try to micromanage government social sector schemes.

VII. In the license era, the Bureau of Industrial Costs and Prices was a repository of industry-specific information. Such an information base is sorely needed today. NITI Aayog can work *in tandem* with the Competition Commission, the Reserve Bank, and 3P India (a body that aims to put *public–private partnerships* back on track) on this front.[2]

The body, rightly informed by the principle of the government being an *enabler rather than provider of first and last resort,* has other messes to sort out. NITI Aayog must live up to its name of handing out an even deal to all. The *niyati* (fate/karma) of the NITI Aayog hinges vitally on how some of these concerns are addressed in the years ahead.

Functions: Being the incubator of ideas for effective governance would be the core mission of NITI Aayog. According to the resolution issued by the government, there are 13 objectives of the new body with a focus on providing the "national agenda."[3] NITI Aayog has a very amorphous agenda. These objectives may be grouped under four major heads:

I. Fostering cooperative federalism by providing structured support to states on a continuous basis

II. Formulating a strategic vision and long-term policies and program framework for both the macroeconomy and different sectors

III. Acting as a knowledge and innovation hub and providing research inputs by undertaking and accessing globally available research

IV. Providing a platform for interdepartmental coordination

Basically, the objectives of the new institution sound very much like those of the Planning Commission as the monitoring and evaluation roles have been retained. According to Pronab Sen (a former principal adviser in the Planning Commission and chairman of the National Statistical Commission), "The only change, perhaps, is that the new body has not been given the powers to allocate funds, but that also needs further clarity. The mandate to look into the interest of national security is new."[4] Nowhere is this more relevant than in the area of energy security where India has failed to evolve a coherent policy over the years. Similarly, networking with other national and international think tanks and with experts and practitioners, as has been envisaged, will add heft to the advice that the NITI Aayog will provide.

The NITI Aayog has been charged with developing a 15-year vision, a 7-year Strategy, and a 3-year implementation framework. NITI Aayog needs to articulate a broader overarching vision and provide the touchstone for gauging their relative importance. Ideally, the vision should be amenable to quantification to a substantial extent so that the technocracy is able to work out the targets, the trade-offs, the time dimensionality, and the strategies that need to be followed. It is not necessary that the vision statement itself must be quantitative in nature—the quantitative dimensions can be worked out through a process of interaction between the planners and the leadership. There have been two pronouncements by Shri Narendra Modi, the prime minister, that have the potential for providing such an overarching vision. The first is the slogan "Sabka saath, sabka vikas" (with all, development for all). This is similar to the "*garibi hatao*" (eliminate poverty) vision in that it is not in itself quantitative but can easily be fleshed out in concrete quantitative terms. The second is the target of doubling farmers' incomes in 10 years (Sen 2017). On getting elected with a sound mandate in 2019, the prime minister said that the government would continue to focus on the poor, but also the minorities, who had been "deceived" so far, who had been made to live in fear and treated as a mere vote bank. It was time to end the trust deficit with them, he declared, and added "Sabka vishwas" (trust of all) to his slogan of "Sabka saath, sabka vikaas." This is an admirable message.[5]

The effectiveness of NITI will depend on how it charts out a course for itself. Despite the claims of a marked departure from the past, the institution has to function in the prevailing milieu and deal with the burden of legacy. NITI Aayog will facilitate grassroots planning; how exactly this will be carried forward needs to be seen. How this operates in practice will bear close watching.

Organizational setup[6]: This was where the role of the vice-chairperson—who would carry cabinet minister rank—was crucial. The vice-chairperson of NITI Aayog would have access to the prime minister, its chairperson, and might thus have a realistic possibility of helping to shape the agenda. The NITI Aayog would have a *three-tier* structure for a specified tenure headed by the prime minister, with a governing council comprising chief ministers and Lt. governors of union territories (UTs), regional councils to deal with issues related to more than one state, and a full-time organizational framework. With a role for states, it was likely to be a more representative body than the Planning Commission. The new body would have a vice-chairperson to be appointed by the prime minister, in addition to four to five full-time members and two part-time members. Four union ministers would serve as ex-officio members. There would also be a chief executive officer (CEO) with a fixed tenure and in the rank of secretary to the government of India. Besides, there would be specific regional councils, while experts and specialists from various fields would be specially invited by the prime minister. The two part-time members would be from leading universities and research organizations. *Regional councils* would address specific issues and contingencies impacting more than one state or a region.

"The success of the institution in achieving interministerial, interdepartmental coordination will depend on the trust and cooperation it receives from them and the harmony with which the Aayog and various ministries work. There could be tensions between the technocrats in the Aayog and various ministers on the one hand, and between the technocrats and bureaucrats on the other. There is also the danger of bureaucratization of the Aayog. Similarly, success in fostering cooperative federalism will depend on the trust of and cooperation from the states. In particular, the first Aayog will have a tremendous task of shaping the character and charting a course to make it an important institution in the Indian federal polity to transform India" (Rao 2015a).

Challenges ahead: Given the complexity of the country—its federal structure, multiparty political system, the growing challenge of minority management, and the issue of poverty before *caste, religion, region, and domicile considerations*—it will be rather too early to predict the Aayog's ability to profile a central policy framework that will create an effective roadmap to guide the political executives of the government. The government had said that the hallmarks of its governance model would be "people-centric, policy driven, time-bound delivery, minimum government, maximum governance." Will NITI Aayog be able to create such a nonpartisan model? (Banerjee 2015). A lot will depend on what use the prime minister who heads the organization will put it to. It would be interesting to see what the new body does and how it relates to other parts like the role of the Finance Commission.

Drawing on six decades of India's experience with planning, the main lesson for the NITI Aayog is that it must devote careful thought to the planning process as to the strategic plan itself. It must recognize that it is not engaged in a technical exercise, but one that involves a deep understanding of people and organizational behavior. The government and the prime minister too must realize that they have to play a significant role in articulating an economic vision, as opposed to endorsing suggestions put up by the bureaucracy. Some of the features of this planning process can be summarized as under (Sen 2017):

I. The prime minister should articulate the broad vision for the country, and not merely endorse a suggestion put up by the bureaucracy.

II. The NITI Aayog should work out the components of this vision in terms of the objectives and targets, and obtain full support of the prime minister. It may also be desirable to place these before the governing council of the NITI Aayog for its endorsement.

COMPOSITION OF NITI AAYOG

The Narendra Modi-led National Democratic Alliance government on Thursday announced the replacement of the 65-year-old Planning Commission with a new institution called Niti Aayog that will ensure greater participation of state governments in policymaking—thus fostering cooperative federalism—and will be more attuned to the nation's contemporary needs.

● FULL-TIME ORGANIZATION

CHAIRPERSON
(Prime Minister)
↓
VICE CHAIRPERSON
(Nominated by PM)
↓
CHIEF EXECUTIVE OFFICER
(Nominated by PM)

FULL-TIME MEMBERS	PART-TIME MEMBERS	EX-OFFICIO MEMBERS
	(Maximum two, from relevant institutions)	(Maximum four, from council of ministers, nominated by PM)

● GOVERNING COUNCIL
Chief ministers and Lt governors of Union territories

● REGIONAL COUNCIL (formed on a need-basis)
Chief ministers and Lt governors of Union territories

● SPECIAL INVITEES
Experts, specialists, practitioners with domain knowledge

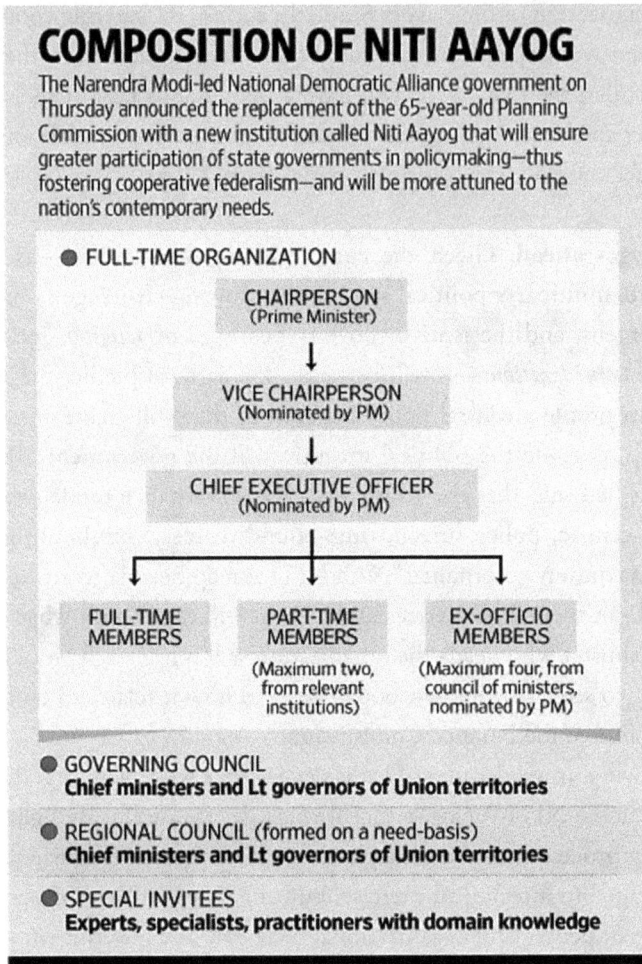

Figure 7.1 Composition of NITI Aayog

Source: MINT, January 2, 2015. Niti Aayog https://www.livemint.com/Politics/3MRK8onj7Ab3nkc9ejoOsN/Planning-Commission-renamed-as-Neeti-Ayog.html (accessed February 6, 2020)

III. The broad strategy for attaining the expanded vision should be worked out within the NITI Aayog, keeping in mind the interrelationships and synergies that may exist among the various objectives. This strategic plan should confine itself to strategy and not extend itself to detailed design, which should be left to the lower tiers. This involves laying out the objectives, the targets, the time path, and the resources. All else is detail, which is best done by others.

IV. In framing the implementation or action plan, the NITI Aayog should clearly specify which interventions should be designed and controlled by the central ministries and which should be left to the state governments with only financial support from the center.

V. In the course of formulating the strategic plan, there will inevitably be serious differences of opinion between the NITI Aayog and the ministries/state governments. These differences need to be resolved before the strategic plan is finalized. The resolution can only be done by the CEO.

VI. Last, but not least, the NITI Aayog should consciously guard against developing hubris, which inevitably leads to micro-prescriptions—the bane of the erstwhile Planning Commission.

The overall efficacy of the NITI Aayog will depend crucially on the quality of experts it can round up to be its members, and also the headroom and space the prime minister gives it to allow it to operate effectively. The new recruits will hopefully bring fresh thinking to economic policy. The problem is the new generation has parachuted to the top. It does not have the nuanced feel of Indian realities needed to design policy. It will have to learn fast. The Aayog's structure will also be relevant. Any enhanced participation from state chief ministers may help the government achieve the prime minister's stated goal of cooperative federalism, but for that to happen, the new governing council has to be more active with regular consultations. Financial decentralization to the lowest tiers of the government for improved efficiency in public goods delivery is essential. In this context, the allocative role that continues to be relevant for a federal entity cannot be entirely divorced from the political process. By Divorcing the allocative role from the Aayog's policy advisory functions will make the Aayog a toothless entity.

Four years of NITI Aayog: The NITI Aayog is the premier policy think tank for the government of India. It has been providing both directional and policy inputs, designing strategic and long-term policies and programs, and has been helping with relevant technical advice to both the center and states since its establishments in 2015. Over the last 4 years, NITI Aayog has played a significant role in shaping many signature policy initiatives, such as the following:

I. Measuring performance and ranking states on outcomes in critical sectors

II. Sustainable action for transforming human capital (SATH)

III. Ek Bharat Shrestha Bharat

IV. Development support services to states (DSSS) for development of infrastructure

V. Public–private partnership in health

VI. Resolution of pending issues of states with central ministries

VII. State Human Development Report

VIII. Transforming of 115 identified aspirational districts

IX. Promoting inclusive growth—giving fillip to the government's goal of "Sabka saath, sabka vikas"

X. Enabling evidence-based policymaking and enhancing productive efficiency with long-term vision

XI. Cross-sectoral interventions

XII. Institutionalizing project monitoring to improve implementation and efficacy of government schemes

XIII. Partnering with national and international organizations and promoting stakeholder consultation in policymaking

XIV. Knowledge and innovation hub

XV. Promoting entrepreneurial ecosystem

XVI. Catalyzing reforms in agriculture

XVII. Promoting adoption of frontier technology

XVIII. International engagements

The prime minister's call for "Sankalp se siddhi" (attainment through resolve) is a clarion call for a radical transformation for a New India by 2022 to 2023, roars the NITI Aayog's "Strategy for New India @75" (2018) document in its introduction. After close to 4 years of the NITI Aayog, by far, this is the most noticeable document from the body. It has a vision for the country, and aligns with the vision of the executive head of state. And, as it claims, the agency consulted over 1,300 experts, both from government and nongovernment agencies, to prepare the blueprint for a new paradigm of development to be achieved in the next 4 to 5 years. The prime minister's articulation of the "new" vision has uncanny similarity to Jawaharlal Nehru's "tryst with destiny" call.

A close review of the NITI Aayog's vision document (Strategy for New India @75) offers valuable insights and suggestions on the real issues that India must face for inclusive growth. It would be good if experts come to talk about the NITI Aayog and chief ministers came to its seat that is, the Yojana Bhavan (New Delhi based headquarter of NITI Aayog). There should also be 3-year action plans and a perspective. The real issue for India is growth across gender, caste, and religious lines, for markets cannot function otherwise. Also, it has to grow fast. The vision document states this but the detail is unfortunately only promised (Alagh 2018).

The tall call for a new deal for India falls flat when one looks into the details of the strategy document. Its drivers for change are employment, economic growth, doubling of farmers' income, and housing for all, besides a boost for the service sector. As one reads the details, one gets the feeling that there is nothing new the Strategy for New India @75 is talking about. For each of these drivers, India is at present facing an upheaval task of bringing in radical changes. There is no doubt about that. But the strategy is not exactly new. It says in generic terms that India needs to increase agriculture growth, raise employment, and reform agricultural markets. These are the same codes that in the 1950s policymakers and the political leadership identified as drivers of growth. And now too they remain the same. But for a country that has not been able to readjust these drivers to make them propel growth, another call for doing the same is more of an acceptance of failure, than a new vision (Mahapatra 2018).

NITI Aayog has been mired in controversies as well, including the decision to release the back series GDP data. Experts questioned the NITI Aayog's role in the new data that showed that growth during the United Progressive Alliance (UPA) government was lower than earlier estimated. **NITI Aayog's governing council meetings**: So far, five meetings of the governing council have been held under the chairmanship of the prime minister.[7]

I. February 8, 2015: laid down the key mandates of NITI Aayog, such as fostering cooperative federalism and addressing national issues through active participation of the states

II. July 15, 2015: reviewed the progress made by the three subgroups of chief ministers and the two task forces

III. April 23, 2017: pitched for conducting simultaneous elections of the Lok Sabha and the state assemblies and shifting to a January–December fiscal year

IV. June 17, 2018: deliberated upon measures taken to double farmers' income and the progress of the government's flagship schemes

V. June 15, 2019: stressing the need to collectively address poverty, unemployment, rain-water harvesting, drought, pollution, pockets of underdevelopment, aspirational districts, transforming agriculture, security related issues with specific focus on left-wing extremists (LWE) districts, and all such factors that constrain India's progress; emphasized the goal to realize the potential of the country, to make a New India by 2022 and a U.S.$5 trillion economy by 2024.

Owing mainly to political differences, Mamata Banerjee (West Bengal chief minister) did not attend the fifth meeting of the governing council of NITI Aayog, on June 15, 2019, saying it is "fruitless" as the body has no financial powers to support state plans and the Aayog is not effective. She also suggested that focus should be shifted to the Inter-State Council (ISC) to deepen cooperative federalism and strengthen the federal polity. Earlier too, Banerjee had skipped meetings of the policy think tank, expressing displeasure over the dissolution of the Planning Commission and creation of a new structure.[8] It seems she has problem with the NITI Aayog; other chief ministers don't have such problem.

An evaluation of working of the NITI Aayog: The NITI Aayog has had an uneven start. It is too early to write it off as a failure. It is useful to remember that it took 6 years before the Planning Commission came into its own with the landmark Second Five-Year Plan in 1956. There is a strong case, however, to rethink the role of the NITI Aayog. The priority is to redefine its tasks against the emerging backdrop of the new fiscal federalism rather than as an investment planning agency.

The NITI Aayog is long on generalities and short on specifics. More than the structure of the new body, the fact that it will function as an enabler for good governance and a performance monitor of various governmental programs and schemes might hold the key to the success of the new body. The end of the Planning Commission and the beginning of NITI Aayog marks a big departure. Care must be taken to ensure the independence of the new body. It should also remain *apolitical* to win the trust of chief ministers. With the prime minister's weight behind it, it should be able to attract the highest talent in the country. How far the government accepts its recommendations also depends on the prime minister. A government's errors affect millions of people for no fault of their own, and hence, must be avoided as far as possible. Churning the issues among thoughtful people is a way of identifying such errors, as also a way of achieving objectives more quickly and economically. The main challenge would be to articulate the vision of the NITI Aayog and in a manner that it becomes relevant to changing times.

What sounds good does not always work out that way. It is not clear what precisely the new mechanism will work *on the ground*. Related to this aspect, the question is raised whether the prime minister is taking on too much himself. Efficient delegation of authority is a hallmark of inspirational leadership. *Niyat* and *niti* (intention and policy) are inextricably intertwined, and the Aayog's functioning is expected to strengthen this in the larger interest of the economic development of India. The working of a new institution can be judged only after it has functioned for a sufficiently long time. The ideas that are claimed to guide the NITI Aayog are sound, but it has to implement them well, and disprove criticism that it is a gimmick.

Kelkar (2019), chairman of the 13th Finance Commission, called for a NITI Aayog 2.0 in his Sukhamoy Chakravarty Memorial Lecture on India's new fiscal federalism. He pitched for the setting up of a "new NITI Aayog" and giving it responsibility for allocating capital and revenue grants to the states. It is desirable that a functionally distinct entity, such as the new NITI Aayog, be put to use to do the job at hand related to structural issues, including removal of regional imbalances in the economy. This doesn't mean that the new NITI Aayog should take the form of the old Planning Commission. The new NITI Aayog will annually need resources of around 1.5 to 2 percent of the GDP to provide suitable grants to the states for mitigating development imbalances. The restructured NITI Aayog will provide a national perspective on policy, which is much needed since individual ministries tend to take only a sectional view.

He emphasized that in order to make the new NITI Aayog more effective, it is essential to ensure that the institution is at the "High Table" of decision making of the government. "This means the vice-chairman of the new NITI Aayog will need to be a permanent invitee of the Cabinet Committee on Economic Affairs (CCEA). Thus, the new NITI Aayog will make available to the highest level of policymaking the knowledge-based advice and provide the national and long-term perspective on the policy proposals. NITI Aayog should strive to be a think tank with "praxis," possessing considerable financial muscle, and devote its energies to outline coherent medium- and long-term strategy and corresponding investment resources for transforming India." (Kelkar 2019). While Kelkar's view is theoretical in nature, policy experts have suggested that many of these may form a sound foundation for NITI Aayog's future. Reddy (2019) has suggested that "NITI Aayog must be reinvented with appropriate stature and given the benefit of constitutional legitimacy, possibly linking it to the Inter State Council (ISC)."[9]

Endnotes

1. FPJ Bureau. January 3, 2015. "A Participative Planning, Now," Editorial comment, *The Free Press Journal*. https://www.freepressjournal.in/analysis/a-participative-planning-now/510888, (accessed April 17, 2019).

2. The Hindu Business Line. January 4, 2015. "A Better Plan, This." https://www.thehindubusinessline.com/opinion/editorial/a-better-plan-this/article6753910.ece.

3. NITI Aayog. n.d. "Functions and Objectives." http://www.niti.gov.in/content/functions, (accessed April 17, 2019).

4. Verma, R. January 2, 2015. "NITI Aayog Replaces Planning Commission; PM to be Chairperson," *MINT*. https://www.livemint.com/Politics/3MRK8onj7Ab3nkc9ejoOsN/Planning-Commission-renamed-as-Neeti-Ayog.html, (accessed April 17, 2019).

5. Hindustan Times. May 27, 2019. "After Sabka Saath, Sabka Vikas, Win Sabka Vishwas': Modi's Message of Inclusion," Editorial Comment. https://www.hindustantimes.com/editorials/after-sabka-saath-sabka-

vikas-win-sabka-vishwas-modi-s-message-of-inclusion/story-6i8 Lo7ve0ibklPOR7E4jqI.html, (accessed April 17, 2019).

6. Constitution. http://www.niti.gov.in/content/constitution-5, (accessed April 17, 2019).

7. The Economic Times. June 13, 2019. "NITI Aayog's Governing Council to Meet on June 15." https://economictimes.indiatimes. com/news/economy/policy/niti-aayogs-governing-council-to-meet-on-june-15/articleshow/69775930.cms?from=mdr, (accessed April 19, 2019).

8. MINT. June 9, 2019. "Mamata Says No to NITI Aayog Meeting, Terms It 'Fruitless'." https://www.livemint.com/politics/news/mamata-says-no-to-niti-aayog-meeting-terms-it-fruitless-1559907554696.html, (accessed April 18, 2019).

9. The Hindu Business Line. March 26, 2019. Refocus scope of Finance Commission, reinvent NITI Aayog with greater powers: Y V Reddy, https://www.thehindubusinessline.com/todays-paper/tp-news/article26649104.ece, (accessed April 20, 2019).

CHAPTER 8

Indian Polity: Fiscal Federalism

This chapter is concerned with union–state financial relations. It spells out the principles governing fiscal federalism; states the provisions enshrined in Indian Constitution related to the division of financial powers between the union and states; explains the role of the Finance Commission (which constitutes a pillar of India's federal structure); appraises the role of Finance Commissions; and evaluates the dimension and nature of issues involved in the contemporary fiscal federalism prevailing in the country.

Introduction: Countries are organized either as "unitary" (France) or as "federations" (India, Brazil, the United States). In the first group, a national or a central government makes the economic decisions for the entire country's territory. In the second group, a constitution has generally assigned various government economic functions between the central government and the subnational government, and to a lesser extent, between the states, or the regions, and the local jurisdictions that operate within them. Generally, large countries such as India, Brazil, the United States, and Australia have chosen a federal structure, one that is assumed to better reflect and satisfy the preferences of citizens in different areas, who may have different cultural backgrounds and economic needs.

In a country as large and as diverse as India, these differences are obviously an important consideration and may require the adaptation of some policies. At the time when the constitutions for federal countries are drafted, it is impossible to anticipate future developments, and thus, the future preferences and needs of the populations. It is, therefore, impossible to allocate, in a permanent and unchanging way, the present and future governments' responsibilities, among the three government tiers. With the passing of time, and with the changing socioeconomic environment of the country and of the world, different needs are likely to arise, needs that were not contemplated at the time when the constitution was drafted.

The new needs will require a different allocation of responsibilities than that described in the constitution. In all the federations now in existence, there are growing conflicts among the different government tiers related to their specific responsibilities. This has become a common experience. In his 1959 classic and influential treatise, *The Theory of Public Finance*, Richard Musgrave assumed that it would be more efficient to allocate the redistribution of income and stabilization of the economy (two recent new government responsibilities) to the central government, leaving much of the allocation of resources (apart from defense spending) to subnational governments. He believed that this allocation of responsibilities would better reflect the governments' controls over national tools, such as tax levels, and the incidence of taxes and public spending. This was the view of just one influential economist, however. The constitutions of many countries, including that of India, do not necessarily follow Musgrave's directive. Over the years, needs that had not been felt in the past have acquired growing importance. This put pressures on the constitutional arrangements determined in the past. For example, both the stabilization of the economy and the redistribution of the economy had not been important objectives in the past, when the tax burden in India had been only 8 percent of the GDP. They became progressively more important with the passing of the years, leading to large increases in tax levels and in public spending. This raised increasing questions on which level of government should determine how to use the additional revenue (Tanzi 2019).

Center–State fiscal relationship: Federalism is an old concept. Its origin is mainly political. It is well known that the efficiency of a government depends on, among other factors, its structure. Fiscal federalism is the economic counterpart to political federalism. Fiscal federalism is concerned with the assignment, on the one hand, of functions to different levels of government, and with appropriate fiscal instruments for carrying out these functions, on the other. It is generally believed that the central government must provide national public goods that render services to the entire population. A typical example cited is defense. Subnational governments are expected to provide goods and services whose consumption is limited to their own jurisdictions. An equally important question in fiscal federalism is the determination of the specific fiscal instruments that would enable the different levels of government to carry out their functions. This is the "tax-assignment problem" that is much discussed in the literature on the subject. In determining the taxes that are best suited for use at different levels of government, one basic consideration is in relation to the mobility of economic agents, goods, and resources. It is generally argued that the decentralized levels of government should avoid nonbenefit taxes and taxes on mobile units (Rangarajan 2019). Articles 268 to 293 of the constitution deal with the provisions of financial relations between Centre and States.

This implies that the central government should have the responsibility to levy nonbenefit taxes and taxes on mobile units or resources. Building these principles into an actual scheme of assignment of taxes to different levels of government in a constitution is indeed very difficult. Different constitutions interpret differently what is mobile and what is purely a benefit tax. For example, in the United States and Canada, both federal and state governments have concurrent powers to levy income tax. On the contrary, in India, income tax is levied only by the central government though shared with the states. Recognizing the possibility of imbalance between resources and responsibilities, many countries have a system of intergovernmental transfers.

Over years, the performance of the central government is judged not only on the basis of actions taken that fall strictly in its jurisdiction but also on initiatives undertaken in the areas that fall in the Concurrent List and even the State List. Today, the central government is held responsible for everything that happens, including, for example, agrarian distress. In viewing the responsibilities of the center and the states one must take a broader view than what is stipulated in the constitution (Rangarajan 2019).

The Planning Commission was replaced by the NITI Aayog, on January 1, 2015 which is simply a think tank with no powers of resource allocation. Perhaps the time has come for the constitution to be amended and the proportion of shareable taxes that should go to the states fixed at the desired level. The shareable tax pool must also include cesses and surchargeas these have sharply increased in recent years. (Cess is a tax on tax, levied by the government for a specific purpose. The education cess, that is levied currently, is meant to finance basic education in the country. Surcharge is an additional burden to the tax being already levied. Generally, surcharge is levied for a certain period of time).

There are issues related to horizontal distribution. Equity considerations have dominated the allocations. This is as it should be. The ability of bringing about equalization across states in India, however, has limitations. Even the relatively richer states have their own problems and feel "cheated" because of the overuse of the equity criterion. An appropriate balancing of criteria is needed particularly in the context of the rise in unconditional transfers. Of course, appropriate balancing is what all Finance Commissions are concerned about (Rangarajan 2019).

Constitutional provisions in India: India is a constitutional republic consisting of 28 states, each with a substantial degree of control over its own affairs; 5 less fully empowered union territories (UTs); and 3 empowered UTs with legislature are the Delhi national capital territory, which includes New Delhi, India's capital, Puducherry, and Jammu and Kashmir. "The three lists contained in the constitution's seventh schedule detail the areas in which the union and state governments may legislate" (Encyclopaedia Britannica). There are also *local authorities* (comprising municipalities, municipal corporations, *zilla parishads*, village *panchayats*, etc.); these are, however, created under statute, and are under the administrative supervision of state governments. Financial relations between the union and state governments are governed by constitutional provisions.

"The Indian Constitution lays down the functions as well as taxing powers of the center and the states. It is against this background that the issues related to the correction of vertical and horizontal imbalances have been addressed by every Finance Commission, taking into account the prevailing set of circumstances. Central transfers to states are not, however, confined to the recommendations of the Finance Commissions. There are other channels as well, like the discretionary grants of the central government" (Rangarajan 2006). The ultimate position appears reasonable. The question may be on the mode of transfers.

Taxing powers: The distribution of taxes in India is more logical and thorough than in other federations. The Concurrent List does not include any sources of taxation. There is, thus, an attempt to avoid all overlapping jurisdiction of taxation. Articles 268 to 281 of the Indian Constitution deal with the distribution of revenue between the union and the states. The Constitution (80th Amendment) Act, 2000 has altered the pattern of sharing of central taxes between the center and the states in a fundamental way.

Grants-in-aid: The constitution expected that the union government would be left with a surplus of funds in relation to the duties it had to discharge, and the states would be deficient of resources in relation to their responsibilities. Provisions were, therefore, made for supplementing the resources of state governments under Article 275(1) of the constitution, as grants-in-aid by the central government. Grant-in-aid is a transfer of money from the union government to state and local governments for the purpose of funding a specific project or program. Grant money is not a loan, and does not have to be repaid, but it does have to be spent according to the central government's guidelines for that particular grant. The actual amounts of grants-in-aid payable each year are to be fixed by the government after considering the recommendations of a Finance Commission.

Federalism is not only a unifying but also a leveling up force. Federal grants-in-aid to the constituent units have been necessary, and this feature exists in all federations. The simple reason behind this is that no system of distribution of financial sources between the federation and the units can possibly meet the needs of national development and social services, which are usually the responsibility of the units. By this device, financially weaker states can be assisted in bettering their economic conditions. The constitution also allows the union and state governments to make grants for any public purpose (Article 282). Article 282 has been kept outside the purview of the Finance Commission. Presumably, it was meant to be used only in an emergency and not for the purpose of making any regular financial assistance.

Borrowings: Article 292 of the constitution empowers the government of India to borrow upon the security of the Consolidated Fund of India, that is, the resources of the union, subject only to such limitations as the parliament by law may impose. The government of India can *borrow internally as well as externally*. States too are empowered to borrow under Article 293. According to this article, a state cannot borrow outside India. The borrowing powers of the states are limited. Furthermore, if a state is indebted to the union (as every state is now), it may not resort to further borrowing without the prior consent of the central government. The state governments do not, regard this provision as putting them unduly in the grip of the union. It does not appear that the working of this article has been detrimental to the interest of the states. This is amply clear by the fact that "in view the Centre's policy for cooperative federalism it has decided to simplify the process of approval of additional borrowing limits requested by States".[1]

The scheme of distribution of resources and of functions makes the *state governments inevitably dependent upon the central financial transfers*, for which the balancing devices have already been provided. The constitutional provisions have avoided rigidity in these balancing devices by leaving undefined the exact quantum of devolution and its distribution among the states. *Basically, the working of center–state financial relations can be seen from the overall result of financial operations on state finances.* The relationship can also be seen in terms of various elements of fiscal federalism such as *sharing of taxes, statutory and discretionary grants-in-aid, and central loans to states.*

Constitutional mandates for local governments: Of late, there is a swing toward fiscal federalism that promotes *democratic decentralization*, which ideally should allow for an optimum equilibrium to be reached through effective citizens' engagement in expressing their preferences and local governments' efficiency in meeting public demands (Oates 1977). "From a minuscule number of 4,841 *Lok Sabha, Rajya Sabha, and state assembly members* representing the country, following the *73rd and 74th Constitutional Amendments* in December 1992, India has today 0.25 million local governments with over three million elected representatives, which makes the Indian federation the largest democratic country with the biggest representative base in the world" (Oommen 2010). *The 73rd Constitutional Amendment designs the following six-layered federal polity*[2]:

I. Gram sabha

II. Gram panchayat

III. Block

IV. District panchayats

V. The state

VI. The union (the apex tier)

The 74th Amendment incorporates the *urban local bodies (ULBs)* into this federal structure. *India is, thus, a multilevel federalism that can be broadly categorized as a functional cooperative federalism.* Articles 243(I) and 243(Y) of the constitution spell out the tasks of the State Finance Commissions (SFCs). They are to review the financial position of local governments. The tasks are strictly patterned on the Union Finance Commission (UFC) as provided for in Article 280 of the constitution. Following the 73rd/74th Amendments, two subclauses were added to Article 280(3) that require the UFC to recommend measures needed to augment the consolidated fund of a state to supplement the resources of the Panchayati Raj Institutions (PRIs) and ULBs in the state "on the basis of the recommendations made by the Finance Commission of the State." Each of the state governments was required to pass legislation appointing PRIs and ULBs. It was stipulated that election to these local bodies should be held within the stipulated period. A separate list of 29 functions for rural local bodies (RLBs) and 18 items for ULBs was placed in schedules and assigned to local governments to implement concurrently with the states. *The sources of finance were also identified for the local bodies.* Each state government was required to appoint an *SFC* to recommend tax devolution and grants to the local governments.

Federalism in India is characterized by the constitutional demarcation of revenue and expenditure powers among the three levels of government. The institutional structure of multilevel provision of public services is shown in Figure 8.1. Below the states there are over a quarter million local governments. Of this about 3,000 are in urban areas and the remaining in rural areas. Rural local governments again are at three levels—*district, taluk* (block), and *village*. The urban local governments consist of municipal corporations in large cities, municipalities in smaller cities and towns, and *notified area committees* in smaller towns. Each of the state governments has devolved powers to levy certain taxes and fees to village *panchayats* and ULBs. The states have also instituted a system of sharing of their revenues and giving grants to ULBs and RLBs. In addition, a number of central sector and centrally sponsored schemes are implemented by the local governments, and the funds earmarked for the purpose are passed on to them by the state governments for implementation.

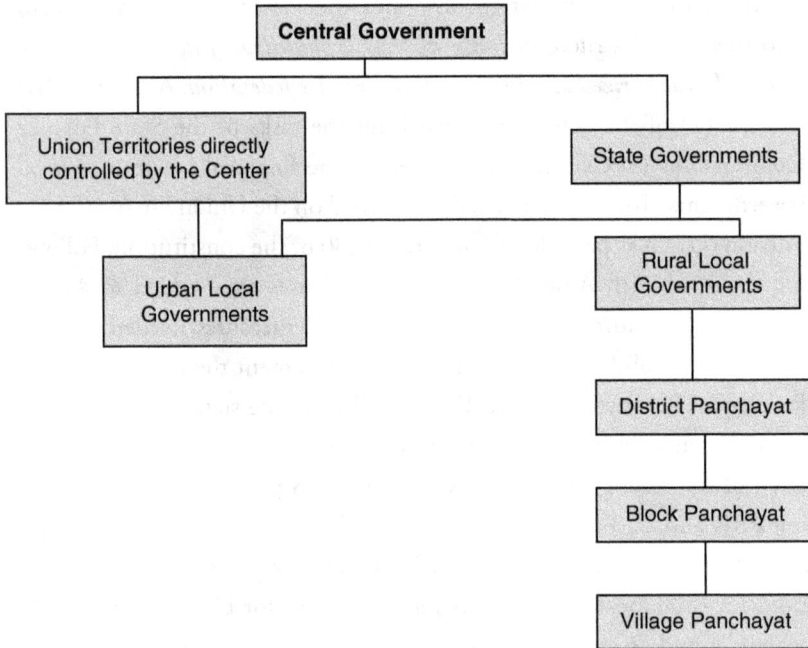

Figure 8.1 Organization of multilevel fiscal system in India

Finance Commission: The percentages of tax receipts to be given to the state governments and the basis of their allocation among the states are not specified in the constitution. All these were left to be decided by a *Finance Commission*. The constitution (Article 280) provides for the appointment of a Finance Commission at the expiry of every fifth year, or at such earlier time as the president considers necessary, to make recommendations to the president as to the following:

A) The distribution between the union and states of the *net proceeds of taxes* that are to be, or may be, divided between them (under Chapter I of Part XII of the constitution) and the allocation between the states of the respective shares of such proceeds
B) The principles that should govern the *grants-in-aid* of the revenues of the states out of the Consolidated Fund of India
C) *Any other matter* referred to the Finance Commission by the president in the interests of sound finance

Thus, in terms of the constitutional provision, a duly appointed *Finance Commission* is entrusted with the task of determining the amounts to be transferred to state governments and of evolving principles for the distribution of such recommended amounts among the state governments. *The provision for the appointment of an independent body for such purposes is a unique feature of the Indian Constitution.* It is meant to provide a measure of assurance to the state governments that the entire problem of financial relationship between the union government and them would be conducted on the basis of a *periodical review and the principles suggested by such an independent body. The element of discretion or arbitrariness in giving financial assistance was meant to be kept under check as a result of this provision.*

The constitution authorizes the Finance Commission to determine their procedure. *The Finance Commission (Miscellaneous Provisions) Act, 1951* has conferred on the commission all the powers of a civil court under the Code of Civil Procedure, 1908. In terms of the 1951 Act, the commission is to be *headed by a person* selected from those who have had experience in public affairs, and the *four other members* are to be selected from among persons who (a) are or have been, or are qualified to be appointed as judges of the high court or (b) have special knowledge of the finances and accounts of the government or (c) have had wide experience in financial matters and in administration or (d) have special knowledge of economics. Every member of the commission is to hold office for such period as may be provided for in the order of the president appointing him but shall be eligible for reappointment.

The *first Finance Commission* was appointed in November 1951; it submitted its report in December 1952, and 14 Finance Commissions have reported so far. The government constituted the 15th Finance Commission on November 27, 2017, with Nand Kishore Singh as the commission's chairman. In the context of the terms of reference (ToR) of the 15th Finance Commission, certain key aspects relate to the following:

A) The mandate for using the 2011 population
B) "Whether revenue deficit grants" be given at all
C) The impact of the goods and services tax (GST) on the finances of the center and the states
D) The reference to "conditionalities" on state borrowing
E) Providing performance incentives with respect to some contentious indicators

The ToR of the 15th Finance Commission has moved away from the more conventional ToRs of the previous Finance Commissions in many respects. The ToR are wide ranging, but there is nothing wrong with that per se. The Commission submitted its interim report on devolution formula for the financial year 2020–21. The final report for the period April 1, 2021 to March 31, 2026 will be submitted by October 30, 2020.[3] The recommendations of the commission will have to come into effect from April 1, 2020. Table 8.1 presents details regarding the years of establishment and reporting of the various Finance Commissions.

Each commission has taken about one to one and a half years to submit its final report. The Finance Commission performs a constitutional function of recommending the distribution of the "divisible pool" of union taxes between the central and state governments. The challenge is to divide fairly and efficiently. The former requires an impartial assessment of the needs of a state, while the latter ensures that the commission does not end up perversely rewarding backwardness. Efficiency also requires rewarding fiscal prudence. Thus, the share is not purely on the basis of tax collection nor on state GDP nor on population. It is a judicious mix of all these factors and more. The challenge before the commission will be to establish the new dynamic of tax revenues share between the center and the state and among the states as well (Rao 2017).

A move toward cooperative federalism: *Cooperative federalism is a two-way street.* If states don't help the center achieve its goals of speeding

Table 8.1 Chronology of Finance Commissions

Finance Commission and period of award	Year of establishment	Year of reporting	Name of chairman
First:1952–1957	November,1951	December 1952	K.C. Neogi
Second:1957–1962	June, 1956	September 1957	K. Santhanam
Third:1962–1966	December,1960	December 1961	A.K. Chanda
Fourth:1966–1969	May, 1964	August,1965	Justice P.V. Rajamannar
Fifth:1969–1974	February, 1968	July, 1969	Mahavir Tyagi
Sixth:1974–1979	June, 1972	October, 1973	K. Brahmananda Reddy
Seventh:1979–1984	June, 1977	October, 1978	Justice J.M. Shelat
Eighth:1984–1989	June, 1982 First Report for 1989–1990	April, 1984	Y.B. Chavan
Ninth:1990–1995 (Second Report)	June, 1987	July, 1988 December 1989	N.K.P. Salve
Tenth:1995–2000	June, 1992	December 1994	K.C. Pant
Eleventh: 2000–2005	July, 1998	June, 2000	Dr. A.M. Khusro
Twelfth: 2005–2010	November, 2002	November 2004	Dr. C. Rangarajan
Thirteenth: 2011–2015	November 2007	December 2009	Dr. Vijay Kelkar
Fourteenth:2015–2020	January 2013	December 2014	Dr. Y.V. Reddy
Fifteenth: 2020–2026	November 2017	October 2020	N.K. Singh

up economic growth, the divisible pie and their revenues will get smaller; if GDP and high-quality jobs don't grow, poverty levels in states can't come down. The cooperative federalism is being practiced since 2014. The "genuine and continuing partnership of states" by replacing the Planning Commission with a National Institution for Transforming India (NITI) Aayog has yet to be tested. India's fiscal architecture is undergoing a radical overhaul coupled with efforts to rationalize and reduce centrally sponsored schemes (CSS). Missing from this rhetoric of decentralization and cooperative federalism is any debate on the future of the *third tier* of India's federal architecture—*local governments*. Despite the constitutional amendments of 1992, local governments have remained marginal players in India's fiscal system (Aiyar and Raghunandan 2015).

But two issues have to be kept in mind. *First,* India still needs a strong central government for national security as well as to provide national public goods. *Second*, state governments should, in the same spirit, transfer more resources to local governments. It will require political vision to manage the creative tension between a strong center and robust local governance. Better attention can be paid to maintaining assets rather than only creating new ones. Use of borrowed resources will also become better as both the central and state governments start focusing more on using fiscal deficit largely for capital expenditure rather than using deficit for meeting revenue deficits (Srivastava 2015). States will also save much energy and resources. The case for the center's intervention in selected areas like health and education was based on the need to achieve minimum common standards across states. With greater autonomy, the states may perform more efficiently. There will certainly be major benefits from federalism in the years to come, especially if the NITI Aayog can play a mentoring and incentivizing role. The creation of the NITI Aayog will radically alter center–state fiscal relations, and further the government's vision of cooperative and competitive federalism. Many questions on the future of the cooperative federalism agenda, however, still remain unanswered. With the plan versus nonplan distinction gone, all union–state devolution now devolves on the Finance Commission, apart from restructured CSS, which no longer have a discretionary template, apart from some special dispensation for North Eastern and Himalayan states and UTs.

Conclusion: India has adopted federalism to actualize and uphold the values of national unity, cultural diversity, democracy, regional autonomy, and rapid socioeconomic transformation through collective efforts. Federalism is a device by which the plural qualities of a society are articulated and protected. A product of historical forces in plural societies, federalism is devised to secure both regional autonomy and national unity. The strength of these regional and national forces changes from time to time, in keeping with changing social, economic, and political conditions and compulsions. Federalism is a principle that defines the relationship between the central government at the national level and the constituent units at the regional, state, or local levels. A well-designed, and more importantly, a well-functioning system of federal governance, by virtue of its manifold benefits, plays a key role in promoting the stability and prosperity of nations, as the heights attained in development by the leading federations of the world—the United States, Canada, Australia, and Switzerland—demonstrate (Singh 2019a).

The ongoing transformation in the country's federal polity is poised to acquire fresh momentum. In the future, the 28 states and 7 UTs are going to be much bigger stakeholders in the country's future than ever before, and this has been made possible by an unprecedented pooling of sovereignty by both the union government and the states. In short, in the future, the sum of the parts will be greater than the whole. The country's polity has taken an unprecedented step by pooling the sovereignty of the center and the states by creating the GST Council—the institution that will drive its own rollout.

Endnotes

1. Centre simplifies approval process for additional borrowing by States, The Hindu Business Line, June 25, 2018. https://www.thehindu-businessline.com/economy/centre-simplifies-approval-process-for-additional-borrowing-by-states/article24255886.ece, (accessed on December 31, 2019).

2. (i) The gram sabha/gram panchayat is the only grassroots-level of panchayati raj formalised local self-governance system in India at the village or small-town level, and has a sarpanch as its elected head. People use the forum of the Gram Sabha to discuss local governance and development, and make need-based plans for the village.
(ii) Block is a district sub-division for the purpose of Rural development department and Panchayati raj institutes.
(iii) Zilla Parishad or District Panchayat, is the third tier of the Panchayati Raj system. Zila Parishad is an elected body. Block Pramukh (head) of Block Panchayat are also represented in Zila Parishad.

3. Finance Commission submits interim report for fiscal 2020–21, The Hindu Business Line, December 5, 2019. https://www.the-hindubusinessline.com/economy/finance-commission-submits-in-terim-report-for-fiscal-2020-21/article30189465.ece, (accessed on December 31, 2019).

CHAPTER 9

Democracy and Development

What is the relationship between democracy and development? Is democracy the best way to achieve economic development? What is the best political system for achieving economic development and enduring prosperity? The answers are not obvious. The road from experience to understanding is not straightforward, and requires rigorous analysis of data. Indians have always believed that democracy is good for development (Sen 1999). This chapter will consider both the normative and the empirical side of these questions. It will argue, first, that democracy is inherently desirable; second, that the empirical record of authoritarian developing states is about as mixed as that of democratic states; and finally, that only democratic institutions give any promise of tilting economic development policies toward the interests of the poor.

Concept of democracy: The institutional sketch of a democratic system is that the polity adopts a constitution that defines maximal political rights and liberties, and defines the status of citizenship. The constitution prohibits the establishment of laws that limit or constrain the constitutional rights and liberties of citizens, or that create inequalities in basic rights among different groups of citizens. The constitution further creates a legislative process through which elected representatives engage in a majoritarian process of debate and legislation. Representatives are elected and can be removed by the electorate, and the legislative process is itself governed by majoritarian voting rules. Legislation cannot contravene the constitution, and a separate supermajoritarian process for revision of the constitution is established. India is the world's largest democracy with exceptional diversity.

Democracy is most likely to emerge and survive when certain social and cultural conditions are in place. The American political scientist Fukuyama (2014) has argued that liberal democracies, with their political freedom and economic success, have three important pillars: a strong government, the rule of law, and democratic accountability. Rajan (2016) would add a fourth: free markets. Both democracy and free enterprise create and thrive on competition. But, whereas democracy treats individuals equally, the free enterprise system empowers them on the basis of their income and assets. It is critical to note, however, that in any democratic society there are some people, especially the minority, who will have their views or opinions overridden by the majority. In this regard, for democracy to prevail fully, there is a need for tolerance and respect for different and opposing opinions. In fact, the very admission that there are some views that are going to be suppressed means that democracy is relative, and therefore, differs from one place to another.

Concept of economic development: Development can be considered as the objective of moving toward a state relatively better than what previously existed. In this regard, development could mean any positive change in life. An important point to note, however, is that development is a process and not a once-off event, since it is considered as a progression from what existed previously. As such, development should always occur and be maintained to ensure that people have a positive change in life. Positive change may include access to better health, higher income, greater individual freedom, more opportunities, better education and housing, as well as a richer quality of life. Thus, development is by definition and practice a radical and commonly turbulent process that is concerned with far-reaching and rapid change in the structure and use of wealth, and which, to be successful, must transform.

Economic development, wherever it occurs, will lead inevitably to democracy. The argument, in its simplest form, runs like this: Economic growth produces an educated and entrepreneurial middle class that, sooner or later, begins to demand control over its own fate. Eventually, even repressive governments are forced to give in (Bueno de Mesquita and Downs 2005). Modernization is a syndrome of social changes; once set in motion, it tends to penetrate all aspects of life, bringing occupational specialization, urbanization, rising educational levels, rising life expectancy, and rapid economic growth. These create a self-reinforcing process that transforms social life and political institutions, bringing rising mass participation in politics, and in the long run, making the establishment of democratic political institutions increasingly likely. Today, we have a clearer idea than ever before of why and how this process of democratization happens (Inglehart and Welzel 2009).

The Indian context: In the context of India's economic development, the basics are provided in the constitution itself. The Preamble calls for justice, social, economic, and political; liberty of thought, expression, belief, faith, and worship; equality of status and of opportunity; and fraternity assuring the dignity of the individual and the unity and integrity of the nation. The Directive Principles of State Policy aim at promoting the welfare of the people by securing and protecting a social order in which justice, social, economic, and political, shall inform all the institutions of the national life. The state shall, in particular, strive to minimize the inequalities in income, and endeavor to eliminate inequalities in status, facilities, and opportunities, not only among individuals but also among groups of people residing in different areas or engaged in different vocations.

Nature-given resources—land, water, forest, and minerals—belong to the people and these must be managed as such. Only then there would be human security and dignity. The development process in India should harness the vital elements—material sufficiency, human dignity, democracy, and participatory governance. Such development would involve equitable change in the community, especially in how resources are used, the functioning of institutions, and the distribution of resources in the community. Balanced development could lead to prosperity and equity.

Democracy and Economic Development

The nexus between democracy and development has been one of the most contested issues. Those in support of the linkage argue that the two—democracy and development—are intertwined and depend on or lead to the other. Opposing views, however, claim that the two concepts are independent of each other, and can easily be achieved without necessarily depending or leading to the other. Democracy offers freedom of choice, everywhere from the polling booth to the supermarket. *But that freedom of choice is hardly a prerequisite for economic growth. On the contrary, it often seems to hinder it.* India has languished under democratic leadership, while Chile and South Korea, both dictatorships until recently, are success stories (Pennar 1993). Authoritarian regimes around the world are showing that they can reap the benefits of economic development while evading any pressure to relax their political control. Nowhere is this phenomenon more evident than in China and Russia. Although China's economy has grown explosively over the last 40 years, its politics has remained essentially stagnant. In Russia, meanwhile, the economy has recently improved even as the Kremlin has tightened its political reins (Bueno de Mesquita and Downs 2005). "Today, capitalism thrives without democracy, as the rapid growth charted by China's communist leaders amply demonstrates. Nor does democracy ensure growth for the world's leading industrialized nations. Many are mired in recession or sluggish recovery, and democratic governments from Italy to Japan have been damaged by scandal and are not delivering growth" (Singh 2009).

Over the near term, authoritarian governments, especially those that offer citizens *economic rights,* such as the protection of private property, can achieve strong results. But while the evidence shows that democracy does not lead to growth, it makes a powerful case that growth leads to democracy. Growth leads to democracy for two reasons: (i) As a small slice of the population is enriched, the rest of the citizens agitate for their fair share at doing better, and (ii) such privilege is granted only in democracies. Then, too, rising incomes at first go toward needed goods and investment, then later toward more and more of what economists call luxury goods, such as higher education. A more educated population tends to demand political and civil rights, and so democratization begins (Heo and Tan 2001).

Authoritarian governments have accomplished economic growth through rigid controls from the center, as South Korea, Singapore, and numerous other regimes have done. But larger nations such as China have decentralized the process, and rapid gains have been achieved. The example of other economically successful dictatorship countries strongly suggests that the push for more freedom will intensify in China. *Only decentralization akin to the federalism that boosted American's early growth is likely to bring about both a growing economy and wider freedom.* All governments inevitably play a role in ordering people's lives, but how they do so is critical in determining not only how free people will be, but also how prosperous. For most economists, less government rather than more is preferable on the grounds that it leaves individualism unhindered and promotes economic efficiency. Few, however, take as extreme a view as Nobel Laureate Milton Friedman, who has been a leading apostle of the minimalist view of government.

In real life, such minimalism does not exist, because as democracies have evolved, their role in determining economic outcomes has deepened. Increasingly, both the size and effectiveness of government is being challenged, and nowhere more so than in developing nations. It is important to note that function, rather than size, defines the government's role in the economy. These days, more and more economists believe that it is politics, policies, and institutions that help or hurt growth. It is these arrangements that are overwhelmingly responsible for economic performance. In developing countries, streamlined regulations are such policy-steps that may encourage new business formation. Similarly, *burgeoning bureaucracies and interests groups* in both developing and industrial nations can throw sand in the economic gears and lead to political paralysis or instability. And political instability is one surefire predictor of poor economic performance. Economic growth and political stability are deeply interconnected (Hussain 2014). The uncertainty accompanying political instability reduces investment and encourages capital flight in developing countries, while among industrialized nations, instability leads to poor policy choices. Growth and prosperity cannot long be sustained in an environment that is undemocratic. The democratic system is an imperfect one, but it is the most desirable one.

Governance is a prerequisite for democracy and development. Development stagnation and obstacles to democratization stem from a failure to undertake the necessary steps for establishing a system of rules that legitimate political choices and political behavior. In short, the elements of good governance provide opportunities for democratization and development in a more sustainable fashion. In this respect, getting politics right means a set of normative and institutional changes that transcend the liberal democratic model. Good governance—in the long run—lays the foundation for a liberal form of democracy. According to Nayyar (2001) "market economy and political democracy cannot and should not be separated from each other as if they constitute two different worlds. In every society, economy and polity are closely inter-twined."

"The essence of the tension between the economics of markets and the politics of democracy must be recognized. In a market economy, people vote with their money in the marketplace. But a political democracy works on the basis of one-person-one-vote. The distribution of votes, unlike the distribution of incomes or assets, is equal. One adult has one vote in politics, even though a rich man has more votes than a poor man, in terms of purchasing power, in the market. This tension may be compounded by a related asymmetry between economy and polity. The people who are excluded by the economics of markets are included by the politics of democracy. Hence, exclusion and inclusion are asymmetrical economics and politics. The distribution of capabilities is also uneven in the economic and political spheres. The rich dominate a market economy in terms of purchasing power. But the poor have a strong voice in a political democracy in terms of votes. And there is a mismatch. Governments are accountable to their people, whereas markets are not. In a democracy, of course, governments are elected by the people. But even where they are not, the state needs legitimation from the people, most of whom are not rich or are poor. The task of reconciliation and mediation is obviously difficult but clearly necessary" (Nayyar 2001).

Svante Ersson and Jan-Erik Lane (1996) come to the conclusion that the interaction between democracy and the quality of life is stable over time. The negative findings are that it has not been possible to establish a stable relation between democracy and economic growth or between democracy and degree of income equality. The other expert opinion comes from Srinivasan (1997); on the basis of an extensive review of the literature on democracy and development, he concludes, "While arguments have been made for and against the instrumental role of political democracy in promoting economic development, neither theory nor empirical evidence supported the arguments that democracies will not be able to raise domestic savings and taxes to the extent required for rapid growth and to avoid diversion of tax revenues to wasteful consumption, etc. Theory and empirical evidence also did not support the hypothesis that authoritarian regimes, regardless of their character, will promote development and avoid waste". The only conclusion that one can derive from theory and evidence is that (Guhan 1998):

I. a market economy, by and large, is the most appropriate form of economic management from the perspective of development, and

II. while democracy is to be treasured for its own sake as a bastion of liberty, and a market economy might make it possible to sustain democracy over extended periods of time, authoritarianism is not necessarily inconsistent with the use of markets for economic management and for promoting development.

Apart from democracy being an intrinsic value, it could have a mutually reinforcing interaction with human development; it has not proved to be an obstacle to growth, fair income distribution, or prudent fiscal management, nor have authoritarian governments necessarily scored better on any of these counts. Besides, an important fact of history should be taken into account, namely, that while authoritarian regimes have coexisted with market economies, democracy has not been able to go along with command systems, which suggests that sustaining democracy could be a good way to insure the stability of market economies as well (Guhan 1998). Issues of democracy and development have an empirical manifestation; since World War II over a 100 nations have undergone a variety of processes of political and economic development. Sirowy and Inkeles (1990) conclude that there is little support for a strong positive causal relation between democracy and development. Przeworski and Limongi (1993) arrived at a similar conclusion. It is reasonable, however, to work on the assumption that democratic institutions are compatible with effective economic development.[1] Acemoglu et al. (2014) have argued that "democracy increases future GDP by encouraging investment, increasing schooling, inducing economic reforms, improving public good provision, and reducing social unrest". In their estimation, there is little support for the view that democracy is a constraint on economic growth for less developed economies.

There is a thought that democracy is a development friendly political system. In a democratic system the authority of the state is elected by the people of that state, so it is expected that the elected authority will focus on development for its people. Sometimes democracy goes against development, and this happens courtesy of "popularism." Many a time the government of a democratic country misuses the country's wealth for earning popularity, as popularity earns votes.

Deficiencies in accountability and checks and balances have led to many democracies degenerating into havens of corruption, where the powerful always triumph. Indeed, the relationship between democracy and development is often problematic; in this sense, developing countries often accuse proponents of democracy of placing the "democratic cart" before the "economic horse." It is argued that democracies have great difficulty in taking rapid and far-reaching steps to reduce structural inequalities in wealth, whether they be based on class, color, ethnicity, religion, or a combination of them.[2]

The main mechanism by which democracy is thought to hinder growth is pressure for immediate consumption, which reduces investment. Only states that are institutionally insulated from such pressures can resist them, and democratic states are not. "In a nutshell, democracy is indeed a key predictor of development. Development, however, can still be achieved through other means." This is aptly stated by President Edgar Lungu of Zambia in June 2017 that "Democracy is a very expensive game, but the people of the country have to decide how best to make democracy a bit cheaper and focus resources to develop the country." (Sikuka 2017). A democracy in name alone is little to celebrate if it does not improve the quality of life of its citizens.

Democracy and Development in India

"India is the largest democracy in the world as its population is second highest only after China. When elections come, it is also the noisiest" (Desai 2019a). In a federal polity like India that co-exist with democracy, constitution mandates policies, laws, and regulations allocated between the center and the states. Such power sharing and decentralization of government has historically proved to be a powerful impetus to growth and development. To be effective in promoting growth, federalism must be "market-preserving." There is more to a form of federalism in the allocation of tax revenues, that tilted towards the centre and assigning more spending obligation to the states. Along with political stability comes flexibility and the opportunity for change. Democracy in India protects whole panoply of individual rights constitutionally. Meanwhile, political parties battle for control. Businesses and individuals compete for profit, advancement, and prestige. And social institutions, from houses of worship to institutions of learning, compete for loyalty and support. Nowhere, but in democracies do such competing interests exist. This juxtaposition of certainty and flux is, ultimately, the best guarantor of economic well-being. A democratic polity cannot long survive in an environment in which there is no economic growth, since different groups would be constantly warring over how to split a pie unchanged in size.

Economic development and its main determinants of success are the quality of institutions and policies of a country. The biggest hurdle facing India are her vested interests, which are very strong, and reform will only succeed if it can break the hold of such vested interests. The problem is how to initiate institutional changes within a democratic framework where the rules of the game are complex and different from those in a more autocratic regime. Politics is different from industry, and the populism of politics is rather obdurate in not obeying the rationalism of economics. Policies are just the short-run forms of institutions, and every society needs a good blend of policies and institutions. According to Nayyar (2001), the Indian experience with democracy and development since independence may be divided into three phases:

I.   From 1947 to 1966 the strategy of development was shaped by a political consensus and characterized by a long-term perspective. The spirit of nationalism meant that there was less need to manage conflict, and there was a conscious effort to accommodate the poor even if it was long on words and short on substance.

II. From 1967 to 1990 India *witnessed a qualitative change in the interaction of economics and politics*. Economic policies and economic development were strongly influenced by the compulsions of political democracy. *Those with a political voice made economic claims on the state*. But the process of mediation and reconciliation had long-term economic and political consequences,

III. From 1991 onward, the country was characterized by an absence of consensus and a presence of short-termism; the economics of liberalization and the politics of empowerment seemed to be moving the economy and the policy in opposite directions. The need for conflict resolution was greater than ever before. But the task had become more difficult. And, strangely enough, the effort was much less.

It was now admitted that the economic policy of the government was leading to the development and growth of an exclusively elitist system. Corrections were required and that can be done only by enabling the government to play a more proactive role. *In sum*, the economics of liberalization and the politics of empowerment represent an unstable, if not volatile, mix. Ultimately, empowerment was a more potent force than liberalization (Nayyar 2001).

According to Bardhan (2010), "More generally, the tension between the participatory and procedural aspects of democracy is the fundamental dilemma of democratic governance and development in India." He further emphasizes that it is democracy that has constantly generated and renewed pressure for welfare programs for the poor, even though "leakages" continue to be excessively high. It has also encouraged rights-based activism in the area of information, jobs on rural public works, food and education, and forest land rights, which, at the least, makes more numbers of poor people politically aware of their entitlements to the benefits of development. It is also the case that all around India some localized green shoots of the positive effects of democratic governance on development are now becoming visible—in social service delivery, in social audits of malfeasance in public programs, in citizen associations demanding better infrastructural facilities, and in some regulatory reforms and measures of fiscal responsibility. There are faint signs that in some areas the electorate has started rewarding the economic performance of their elected leaders. In the context of democracy and development in India, the challenge is to "live without illusions, and yet not to be disillusioned."

Despite political difficulties and uncertainties often plaguing India, the country's vibrant democratic structure is a help rather than a hindrance to economic growth. January 24, 2010, marked the diamond jubilee of the Election Commission of India. Elections have become India's institutionalized "political common sense."[2] "India has strengthened its political democracy by giving constitutional sanctity to the Panchayati Raj in rural and municipal bodies in urban areas, creating 0.3 million elected units of local self-government to which have been elected no less than 3.2 million members, as many as 1.2 million of whom are women and 86,000 of whom hold office as president or vice president of their respective local bodies" (Sardana 2010).

Indian voters have realized the power of their votes. In contemporary India, voters understood that they could now evict nonperforming governments and retain performing ones. As a result, political parties are concentrating on governance and development by focusing not so much on caste and religion as on class and regional factors (Kadekodi 2015). The reduction of the voting age from 21 to 18 in 1988.[3] appears to have reduced the impact of such appeals in the form of class and regions in comparison to those of giving opportunities and building capabilities, be it for education, health services, improved living conditions, or enhancing livelihoods. Many state governments such as Bihar, Jharkhand, Odisha, West-Bengal have responded by spending increasing sums on economic and social projects. These expenditures have certainly added to people's well-being.[4]

But corruption, greed for money and power are not good for India's democracy. Rao (2015) has stated that "corruption has entered the judiciary as well. Elections have become increasingly expensive and the preserve either of the wealthy or the corrupt or of those willing to repay for the investment they have made in the process of winning the election". "The problem is not democracy or universal suffrage. It is the ability of politicians and bureaucrats to design schemes for government spending in a way that makes theft of funds possible." "India must do away with the discretionary powers of the government, establish transparent mechanisms for government spending, and drastically reduce the role of the public sector."

One must realize that democracy essentially is a consensus-building process on issues of contemporary concern. Every government has to function in the public interest. A policy implementation framework has to result in the widest good. Even discretion has to be in the public interest, which has to reflect the widest good. India's progress will come through the implementation of laws and never through exceptions to the laws. It is well to remember that democracies have given enduring and prosperous economies (Liberhan 2015).

According to Rajan (2016), while strong institutions—an independent judiciary, opposition parties, press freedom, and a vibrant civil society—prevent government excess, India's "checks and balances" require what might be called a "balance of checks." For example, India must not have an appellate process so slow that it halts necessary government measures. The most heartening development is that more people across India are becoming equipped to compete, and more of the young entrepreneurs are unwilling to kowtow to the government as a matter of course. If India is to have prosperity and political freedom, it must also have economic inclusion and a level playing field. Access to education, nutrition, health care, finance, and markets for all its citizens is a moral imperative, precisely because it is a precondition for sustainable—and democratic—economic growth.

The mere abidance by the ritual of going to elections periodically does not make for a vibrant democracy. India has achieved much through its democracy but it has many more miles to go. There are three challenges that must be taken note of:

I.   "The quality of elections in the "third tier" of government, in village and urban bodies, must be improved to get democracy to the grassroots.
II. Political parties must become democratic internally.
III. Money in elections is distorting democracy. Huge amounts of money are required to campaign nowadays" (Maira 2010). The increasing amounts of money flowing to the media for advertisements and even paid editorials add to the distortion of the process of democracy and election.

"The quality of the public discourse in India, whether within elected bodies like the parliament or in the media, is deteriorating. The other challenge is to improve the delivery of public services. For India, the choice is not between democracy and results. India must have both. Therefore, it requires models of governance and management that will produce results through democratic processes. Consensus building and management are teachable and learnable skills" (Maira 2010).

"Some scholars argue that democracy is needed to keep a multiethnic, multilingual, multicultural, and multireligious country like India intact.

India's rapid economic growth in the context of a democracy is on the whole without parallel. Democratic incumbency is, however, a significant drawback to Indian development. Politics in India has become more consensual and less elitist but at the same time more corrupt and self-serving. Coalition and patronage politics of social factions have combined to make government expenditure a variable outside political control."[5] India wants better economic opportunities (employment), well-being (health care), quality of life (drinking water, road, and public transport), and security (police and women empowerment). "Urban India also desires a better city life with environmentally conscious urban governance (less traffic and pollution), and rural India is looking for solutions that will fix the slump of growth that the agriculture sector in India faces today (access to water and electricity, availability of loan and subsidies, higher price realization)" (Raj and Sastry 2019).

Given the diversity of its languages, religion, ethnicity, and culture makes India the most diverse country in the world, steering a democracy on the development road is no different from driving a car. It is clear that a crisis of governance afflicts India. Establishing a strong sense of credibility in the government and developing adequate capacity for enforcement must be addressed to ensure the success of India's democracy. The purpose of the food security program was to reduce misery, but the program was also good for India's economic growth and democracy. Overall, health reform will probably make India richer as well as more secure. Being nice to the wealthy and cruel to the poor is not the key to economic growth and also not good for the success of democracy. On the contrary, making the economy fairer would also make it richer. Paul Krugman has opined, "Goodbye, trickle-down; hello, trickle-up." [6]

Conclusion: Elections in India, the world's largest democratic exercise in terms of the number of voters, are a validation of the hypothesis that with all their faults, democracies deliver the best results in terms of economic growth over the long term (Vembu 2019). Democracy, at times, can be the sum of contradictory pressures. People will never stop thinking about themselves and their societies in identity terms. But people's identities are neither fixed nor necessarily given by birth. Identity can be used to divide, but it can also be used to unify. That, in the end, will be the remedy for the populist politics of the present (Fukuyama 2019). A democratic polity accords to a popular mandate its highest honor. The debate on the threat that populism poses to democracy has been kindled once again, this time by the 46th chief justice of India. On June 20, 2019, addressing, chief justices and judges of nations that constitute the Shanghai Cooperation Organization, Ranjan Gogoi argued that the erosion of the edifice of law can begin with surging populism; the consequences of this cannot be desirable for democracy.[7] The National Democratic Alliance, which has been reelected in May 2019 with a stronger mandate, has had a history of friction with the judiciary, insisting that the executive have a role in the appointment of judges.

The basic human desire for individual freedom, which is central to the promise of liberal democracy, lives on in different forms within different political cultures. The world's strongmen are unlikely to change that (Bremmer 2019). A country as large and as diverse as Europe, with as many religions as one can wish for, plus the multicolored, rich Hinduism, has never been conquered by a single ruler. It was democracy that unites the Doab and Punjab with Bengal and Assam plus the South. No region, no language can ride roughshod over others. Democracy allows disputes and complaints to be resolved peaceably. "India has set up mechanisms for reconciliation, such as federalism with the statutory Finance Commission, a judiciary that is unitary, and the Election Commission holding regular elections where millions express their voice. Even over the last 72 years, there have been deep divisions in the country but democracy has provided the answer" (Desai 2019b).

In this context, it is well to remember the big unqualified emergence of the Goods and Services Tax (GST) Council as India's first federal institution—genuinely federal and fully functional. Maybe India can bring about a balance between the vote bank equations leading to the flowering of democracy and growth (Sardana 2010). "India has, over the decades, emerged as a leading light in the democratic world on two counts—the masses here have proven their ability to oust well-entrenched regimes from power and have demonstrated their wisdom in opting for clean governance, assurance of development, and national stability and security. And this has happened in spite of that typically Indian social phenomenon of caste and creed affinities ruling the political turf".[8]

Endnotes

1. Umich. n.d. "Democracy and Development." http://www-personal
.umd.umich.edu/~delittle/Democracy%20and%20development
.pdf, (accessed April 20, 2019).

2. A new triangle: India, China and the US. https://www.india-seminar.com/2006/557/557%20ashutosh%20varshney.htm, (accessed on February 6, 2020).

3. The Constitution (Sixty-First Amendment) Act, 1988. http://legislative.gov.in/constitution-sixty-first-amendment-act-1988, (accessed on January 1, 2020).

4. Social Sector Expenditure of States Pre & Post Fourteenth Finance Commission (2014-15 & 2015-16), 2019, NITI Aayog, New Delhi. https://niti.gov.in/sites/default/files/2019-07/Social%20Sector%20Expenditure%20of%20States_%20Paper.pdf, (accessed on January 1, 2020).

5. Assessing Development And Democracy In India Politics Essay. https://www.ukessays.com/essays/politics/assessing-development-and-democracy-in-india-politics-essay.php, (accessed on January 1, 2020).

6. Komlik, O. August 9, 2014. "Paul Krugman: 'Inequality is a Drag… Goodbye, trickle-down; hello, trickle-up.'" *Economic Sociology and Political Economy.* https://economicsociology.org/2014/08/09/paul-krugman-inequality-is-a-drag-goodbye-trickle-down-hello-trickle-up/, (accessed April 22, 2019).

7. Editorial Board. June 21, 2019. "Chief Justice Gogoi Is Right to Highlight the Growing Distance between the 'Public Will' and the Judiciary," *The Telegraph.* https://www.telegraphindia.com/opinion/chief-justice-ranjan-gogoi-is-right-to-highlight-the-growing-distance-between-the-public-will-and-the-judiciary/cid/1692812, (accessed July 17, 2019).

8. Democracy on test (Comment: Spy's Eye), Business Standard, March 24, 2019. https://www.business-standard.com/article/news-ians/democracy-on-test-comment-spy-s-eye-119032400088_1.html, (accessed January 1, 2020).

CHAPTER 10

The Economic Policy Regime in India Prior to 1991

The Indian economy struggled during its initial stages after independence. Due to many political, societal, and personal hindrances, the economy was stagnant. It took many years for the economy to stand up and work for itself. The postindependence period (1950 to 1990) was a very critical time for the country. It includes various steps that were important for the betterment of the country. In this chapter a bird's eye view of important economic decisions taken between 1950 and 1990 has been presented. The rapid economic development strategy of postindependent India had been one of self-reliant industrialization under centralized investment planning. It had emphasized basic and heavy industries and adopted public sector as a major instrument in the institutional framework of a mixed economy where private ownership of means of production was permitted in a democratic political setup. India had a major setback in her planning process when she turned inward following the BoP crises from 1956 to 1957. The explicit strategy of an import substitution (IS) was desired then, reflecting the economic logic of export pessimism that characterized the thinking of Indian planners. Domestically driven import-substituting industry needed cheap imports for the manufacture of goods for the Indian market. Industry was averse to the rise in import prices consequent upon the devaluation.

Under this strategy, the activist state, acting on behalf of the society, assumed heavy responsibility of not only initiating economic development, which the private sector was deemed unwilling or unable to undertake, but also shaping the entire pattern of investment. The direct involvement of the state in economic development resulted not only in heavily regulated markets and private economic activities in a functioning market economy but also in a significant extension of the public sector into diverse economic activities going well beyond the traditional economic rationale provided by market failures.

The activist state needed to transfer financial resources from private savers to itself in order to finance its own expanded activities as also to finance private sector activities in the priority sector. Initially, indirect taxes (excise and customs) were used as instruments to mobilize resources while allocation of private investment was sought to be controlled through industrial licensing. Later, commercial banks were nationalized in 1969 to acquire control over private savings in the form of bank deposits. The instruments of administered interest rates and progressive hike in cash reserve ratio (CRR) and statutory liquidity ratios (SLR) were used to transfer the private savings to the government. These were rechanneled through publicly owned term-lending institutions to finance investments in PSEs and government approved private corporate investments. Apart from keeping the administered interest rate artificially low in order to induce private investment, the activist state enacted labor legislations to protect the interest of the industrial workers.

In view of the aforementioned, the evolution of the postindependence economic policy can be grouped under three broad categories:

I.   Direct, discretionary, and quantitative controls on the private sector
II. Extension of the public sector
III. Rigid regulation of the external sector: foreign capital and trade policy

These features interacted in the institutional setup of functioning markets and private ownership of means of production to generate perverse incentives that constricted the operation of market forces and private economic agents.

Direct, Discretionary, and Quantitative Controls on the Private Sector

In general, controls were operated by the Industrial Licensing Committee, the Import License Committee, the Foreign Collaboration Committee, and the Capital Issues Committee and also involved the Directorate General Technology Development (DGTD) for "indigenous angle clearance." Although much of the personnel of the committees were the same, for most of the period, they met separately as the application went through the various stages of clearance. Needless to say, it was an involved and time-consuming process. A license refers to a written permission granted by the government to a firm that mentions what product can be manufactured by the firm. Further, license also includes various other particulars such as the place where factory is to be located; what products are to be produced; what is the maximum quantity that can be produced; and what are the conditions for the expansion of production. The government resorted to the licensing system so that it could maintain control over industries as per the Industries (Development and Regulation) Act, 1951. The stated objectives of the licensing policy were as follows:

I. Regulate the industrial sector, particularly the private sector, in the desired direction as per the objectives of the five year plans.
II. Check the concentration of ownership of industries in a few hands.
III. Emphasize balanced regional development.
IV. Encourage small-scale industry.
V. Encourage new entrepreneurs to set up industries.

Licensing regime means regulations and accompanying bureaucracy, which means red tape imposed substantial administrative burden, and there was no certainty that an application for a license would be approved within a timeframe or in what timeframe. Entrepreneurs needed to deal with various government departments and officers. The stated objective was to increase industrial production but on the ground it restricted expansion, production of new articles, and so on. Similarly, the stated objective was to check the concentration of economic power in a few hands, but actually it didn't succeed. An undue concern with the problem of monopoly has prevented an economically sensible expansion of the industrial sector, by holding back the expansion of firms that could utilize economies of scale. New licenses were granted to big houses thanks to all the pervasive corruption. They were also allowed to grow at the expense of new players. Bribery was a culture in the "license raj." For bribes, licenses were issued in areas reserved for the public sector or for small-scale industries.

Life under license raj was characterized by scarcity of resources. The specialty of license raj was that licenses were themselves made a commodity, and a scarce one, at that. Hence, if a company wanted to expand production, it needed a license to do so, which was not easily available. A "market" for licenses developed; licenses had a price. Business competition under the license raj meant getting licenses before competitors. Often businesses acquired licenses, not to produce, but to stop the other from expanding. Given this situation, entrepreneurs used to say that the art of managing government relationships was most critical to business success (Agarwal 2016).

The licensing procedure did not enable the government to economize on the use of imports but had quite perverse effects. The licensing system led to a loss of government revenue, at least potentially. The objection to the policy that was pursued is really that the government was neither consistent in the criteria it followed nor did it devise a system that had the capacity to operate efficiently. It is difficult to escape the conclusion that both the economic strategy and the chosen instruments of economic control largely failed to tackle the problems facing the economy.

To sum up, the following criticisms have been leveled against the licensing procedure:

I. There was a lack of clear guidelines.
II. There were *long delays* in the process of approving or rejecting applications.
III. *No systematic rules* were followed to implement the objective of locational dispersion of industry.
IV. The system did not *succeed in controlling the growth of monopoly and reducing the concentration of economic power in industry.*
V. The government was neither consistent in the criteria it followed nor did it devise a system that had the capacity to operate efficiently.

Private sector: Private industrial activity was sought to be guided toward socially desirable activities under the Industries (Development and Regulation) Act, 1951. The important policy instruments used for this purpose included industrial licensing, controls over capital issues, price and distribution controls, and restrictions on foreign collaborations as well as imports of technology. The government nationalized private sector assets in areas such as insurance, banking, coal, and wheat, as well as significant parts of the steel industry. Large industrialists in the private sector were controlled stringently through the Monopolies and Restrictive Trade Practices (MRTP) Act, 1969, in relation to the quantities and types of goods they could produce.

Controls unintentionally offered incentives to *divert resources to directly unproductive rent-seeking activities aimed at preempting the entry of potential competitors.* The resulting noncompetitive markets did not offer incentives for improving productivity or quality. Thus, the private industrial units had neither the freedom to adjust to market signals nor incentives generated by competition to improve efficiency. Controls did not lead to "planned" allocation of private investment either. The Indian economy saw the growth of industries during the mid- and the late 1970s. It was clear back then that India would never be able to master and transcend this sector of the economy because the industrial sector requires technological advancements, intellectual theories, and finances. Since India lacked all those, it was inevitable that the economy cross over this sector and move directly to the service sector. Due to the large population, service providing was far more promising than industrial success. The following were some of the most prominent features of the Indian industrial sector between 1950 and 1990.[1]

    I. Lack of technical knowledge
   II. Excess of obsolete techniques and machinery
  III. Lack of sufficient finances to acquire advanced machinery
  IV. Provision of a lot of employment opportunities
   V. Poor contribution to the national income
  VI. Intense regional imbalance and dissatisfaction among workers

One may summarize the failure of discretionary control as follows:

    I. Disincentive for investment and entrepreneurship
   II. Growth retarded for a variety of reasons; industries struggled for funds for investment either directly or through banks
  III. Corruption and favoritism
  IV. Failure of the delivery system

Labor legislation: Businesses had to have government approval for laying off workers and for shutting down. The Industrial Disputes Act 1947, protects less than 10 percent of India's workforce in a manner that makes it very difficult to retrench unionized workers.

Extension of the Public Sector

The emphasis of the Second Five-Year Plan (1956 to 1961) was on government-led industrialization. The public sector must grow not only absolutely but also relatively to the private sector. The whole picture on control mechanisms that were in place was meant to augment the growth of the public sector. In order to enable the *activist state* to guide the course of development toward socially desirable goals, the Industrial Policy Resolutions of 1948 and 1956 reserved strategic domestic industries, and government monopoly was established in armaments, atomic energy, railroads, minerals, iron and steel industries, aircraft, manufacturing, shipbuilding, and telephone and telegraph equipment. This extended the boundary of the public sector activities beyond those justified by the perceived market failures, namely, electricity; telecommunications; rail, road, and air transport network; and other public utilities. Over the years, the central and state governments formed agencies and companies engaged in finance, trading, mineral exploitation, manufacturing, utilities, and transportation, like Hindustan Insecticides, Ashoka Hotel Corporation, Tyre Corporation of India, Air India, Gas Authority of India Limited (GAIL), Steel Authority of India Limited (SAIL), Oil and Natural Gas Corporation (ONGC). Thus, the government built new state-owned enterprises as diverse as jute mills, hotels, and steel plants.

Public sector units were expected to operate efficiently and generate resources for further investment. Instead, they were saddled with the multiplicity of often-conflicting objectives; had to accept politically driven inappropriately administered prices for their products and services; and were subjected to *bureaucratic and political interference*, which made their efficient operation difficult. They also faced the "soft-budget constraint" with neither penalty for losses nor rewards for efficient functioning. The poor performance of public sector units had a multiplier effect through inefficient, low-quality, and often irregular and fluctuating supplies of infrastructure services and universal intermediate inputs (like iron and steel and financial services), which partly contributed to the inefficiencies of the private sector units. At the macro level, they became a drain on the exchequer through their recurring losses instead of generating resources for investment.

Over and above, some of the important policy measures extending the scope of the public sector were as follows:

I.   In 1956: life insurance business nationalized
II. In 1969: large commercial banks nationalized
III. MRTP Act, 1969: designed to provide the government with additional information on the structure and investments of all firms with assets of more than Rs. 200 million in Indian currency, to strengthen the licensing system, decrease the concentration of private economic power, and place restraints on business practices considered contrary to public interest
IV. In 1973: general insurance business nationalized

The rationale for a large public sector producing capital goods no longer held since in an open economy there was no equivalence between the size of the capital goods sector and the investment rate. But the economy had been resilient.

External Sector: Rigid Foreign Capital and Trade Policy

India's policy regime was complex and cumbersome. There were different categories of importers, different types of import licenses, alternate ways of importing, and so on. The importers were broadly grouped into three categories: (a) *actual users of industrial products and nonindustrial products*, (b) *exporters*, and (c) *others*. The actual users in the first category included enterprises/persons who used to get import license for items earmarked for their own use and not for further sales. These users were entitled to various types of import licenses and could import goods and commodities under these modes alone. Different types of licenses that used to be issued in the pre-reform period can be categorized as (a) *open general license (OGL)*, (b) *automatic license*, (c) *supplementary import license*, and (d) *import through government-owned canalized agencies*. In the OGL category the components and spare parts required by importers were usually imported to India on the basis of this license. These imports were used by the importers in their manufacturing activities. The list of such products that fell under OGL, Restricted Items List, and Banned List used to be released by the government in their annual export–import policy (Mehta 1997).

The instruments used were often extremely complex and detailed and had undergone changes from time to time. The formal nature of an instrument and the way in which it was actually deployed might also be different. Moreover, quite an *elaborate institutional structure* had also been built up for the administration of some of these rules. Whatever the merit and demerits of the economic strategy that has been pursued by the government, its implementation had been very poor. The failure of implementation can be observed at both an aggregative and at the specific sectoral or project level. The most critical failures at the aggregative level are, perhaps, the failure to achieve the planned rates of investment and of domestic resources mobilization, with its consequent continued dependence of foreign aid.

The license raj created a scarcity of foreign reserves. The balance of payment crisis arose in the 1970s and worsened toward the end of the 1980s. India followed a protectionist policy and adopted different instruments. These instruments, to a large extent, were dictated by the objectives of the protectionist policy. The principal objectives of this protectionist policy were as follows:

A) Stabilize balance of payments
B) Encourage industrialization
C) Fulfill the objectives of self-reliance
D) Help in reallocation of resources
E) Provide budget revenue
F) Increase employment

The selection of instruments adopted for achieving the objectives of the protectionist policy can be classified in two broad groups: (a) *tariff* and (b) *nontariff measures*. These instruments were basically used to bring about changes in price, volume, or other parameters related to tradable commodities and services. The import and export policy determines in great detail the import procedures that are applicable to specific products, license, importers' entitlement, as well as other details relevant for the imports of goods and commodities by different categories of importers. India's import and export policy was guided by the *Import and Export Control Act* of 1947. In 1977, two additional orders, that is, the Import Control Order and Export Control Order, were introduced and the subsequent annual policy of import and exports was based on these legislations. *A long-term trade policy, for 3 years, was announced in 1985* by the government and some concrete steps toward liberalization were taken within the framework of economic reforms (Mehta 1997). Licensing system and controls had virtually shut off imports with high tariffs, low import quotas and outright banning of import of certain products. For example, the import tariff for cars was around 125 percent in 1960. India in 1985 had the highest level of tariffs in the world. Nominal tariff rates as a percentage of values in 1985 were 146.4 percent for intermediate goods, 107.3 percent for capital goods, 140.9 percent for consumer goods, and 137.7 percent for manufacturing goods.[2]

Import substitution policies proved to be inefficient. Policymakers were convinced that the basic model of import substitution needed a change. The overall trade regime remained severely protectionist. Tariffs remained high and the effective rates of protection did not fall in the 1980s. Also, there was no drop in the percentage of manufactured imports subject to nontariff barriers (Kotwal and Wadhwa 2011). The Foreign Exchange Regulation Act (1974) reduced the power of multinational corporations by reducing the foreign equity participation of foreign companies from 51 percent to 40 percent. This meant that multinationals would have fewer powers in company boards. This ultimately led to the departure of companies like Shell, Coca Cola, IBM, and Caltex.

Consequences: The strategy of *self-reliant industrialization* that has been characterized as "economic nationalism" resulted in a restrictive trade policy regime that had the same elements as that of the *Nurksian strategy of import substitution-driven industrialization*. This has been achieved by keeping the exchange rate overvalued, which *discriminated against exports*, and using tariffs and quotas on imports as instruments to contain the resulting excess demand for foreign exchange. The import requirements of basic and heavy industry–oriented industrialization put further *pressure on the balance of payments and resulted* in progressively more restrictive controls on imports of commodities and capital and perpetual shortage of foreign exchange in the face of nonexpanding exports.

The government attempted to *close the Indian economy to the outside world. The Indian currency, the rupee, was inconvertible and high tariffs and import licensing prevented foreign goods reaching the market.* India also operated a system of central planning for the economy, in which firms required licenses to invest and develop. The labyrinthine bureaucracy often led to absurd restrictions—up to 80 agencies had to be satisfied before a firm could be granted a license to produce, and the state would decide what was produced, how much, at what price, and what sources of capital were used. The government also prevented firms from laying off workers or closing factories. The central pillar of the policy was import substitution, the belief that India needed to rely on internal markets for development, not international trade—a belief generated by a mixture of socialism and the experience of colonial exploitation. Planning and the state, rather than markets, would determine how much investment was needed in which sectors.

The complex structure of differential indirect tax rates as also administered interest rates and labor legislation led to distortions in relative product and factor prices and resulted in not only inefficient allocation but also misallocation of resources out of line with relative scarcities of capital and labor. The Indian government used the public sector dominated financial system as an instrument of public finance with a complex set of regulations on fixed deposit and lending rates, and channeled credit to the government and priority sectors at below market rates. All these amounted to tax on financial intermediation, which not only reduced the allocative efficiency of intermediation but also resulted in the loss of efficiency and lower real growth of the economy at 3.5 percent per annum despite the doubling of the rates of domestic savings and investment over the 30-year period 1950 to 1980.

These regulations made maximization of working capital and cash–credit loans and project financing as the primary objectives of banks and financial institutions. *Monitoring debtors and recovering loans got low priority encouraged by budgetary support.* As a result, lending occurred with inadequate project appraisal and favored companies established *in line with government dogmas, and loan amounts did not have any relation with perceived risks and expected returns.* In addition, there was no uniform system of accounting practices, no provisioning for nonperforming assets (NPAs), and no valuation of securities held in the bank.

The failure of particular targets of industrial output to be reached during the planned periods, as well the delays in completing various industrial projects on target. Critical shortfalls in the production of steel, fertilizers, and other input continue to be a feature of economic life in India. The failure of public sector industries to reach their investment and output targets has been amply documented in various reports (Agarwal 2016).

The failure of implementation at both the macro- and micro-levels is obviously not unrelated. It has to be borne in mind that the Indian economy is not a centrally planned economy but a mixed economy, with the government having direct control over that small part of it that constitutes the public sector. While some of the criticisms that have been leveled against the government economic policy tend to give the picture of a distinctly *dirigisme* regime, in fact, the government has used both macro- and micro-levels related allocative policy, with greater emphasis on the later.

It has been recognized that the Indian economy suffers from severe structural imbalances and discontinuities between sectors. The characteristic tendency of the government is to try to manipulate the outcome of an economic process without being able to influence the major forces behind that outcome. For the nonagricultural sector, the government has tried to operate two distinct types of control, both of which can be said to belong to the type that bypasses the price mechanism. The tendency of the government is to undertake unnecessarily wide and detailed controls that its administrative capacity cannot handle. While great emphasis is laid on all these objectives, in practice, the operation of the policy has probably been most influenced by the need to conserve foreign exchange.

Beginning of liberal policies: The trajectory of economic policies favoring India's growth was path dependent. From 1947 to 1975 the policy consensus favored an important role of the state within a relatively closed economy. Private enterprise survived during this period but India's trade declined. Changes in the policy consensus favoring economic deregulation began to appear in the mid-1970s, which prepared the ground for the tectonic policy shifts beyond 1991. Path dependence ensured that new policy ideas building upon the lessons of the past took quite some time to get embedded within politics and result in policy outcomes. This is a story of how powerful social actors who derive benefits from a certain set of policies oppose a change in the social equilibrium. Financial crises were critical for the major policy shifts in India. They aided the convinced technocracy and the executive to overcome political opposition to policy change. It became clear to the policy elite that the promotion of Indian agriculture and the private sector was critical in the context of hard budget constraints in 1966 and in 1991, respectively. The financial crises of 1966 and 1991 are critical for explaining India's green revolution in the early 1970s and its tryst with globalization in the 1990s (Mukherji 2009).

The intellectual impetus for deregulation came from the weight of reports commissioned by the government over several decades. From the 1960s on, there was a large body of work within the government in response to the dissatisfaction with the licensing regime. The Indian development strategy recognized the significance of a liberal trade policy in the early 1980s, which was manifested in the form of a number of important recommendations made at that time by several committees. The notable ones focused on a shift in emphasis from control to deregulation through simplification of the import licensing system (Alexander Committee 1978), clear recognition of dynamic comparative advantages associated with export growth (Tandon Committee 1980), the need to harmonize foreign trade policies with other macroeconomic policies, advantages of an export-led growth strategy, a phased reduction in effective protection (Abid Hussain Committee 1984), and the need to discourage inefficient import substitution (Narasimham Committee 1985). Notwithstanding these concerns, the trade regime continued to be characterized by a licensing system that together with a high tariff structure protected the economy from external competition. In addition, the trade performance was constrained by restrictive foreign investment policies (RBI 2003).

The success of East Asian economies had made the government more receptive to the aforementioned recommendations. When a new government came to power in December 1989, there was a renewed focus on industrial reforms. There undoubtedly was some liberalization. The result of such thinking was to reorient economic policies. The roots of the liberalization program can be traced to the late 1980s, but the reach and force of the reform program was rather limited. Some industrial deregulation favoring the Indian private sector was achieved. The telecommunications sector was moved in the direction of private sector orientation. Parts of the Department of Telecommunications (DOT) were corporatized into the government-owned corporate entity Mahanagar Telephone Nigam Limited (MTNL). Since 1991, the Indian economy has been constantly undergoing drastic economic reforms. These reforms have resulted in a shift from the inward-oriented policy of the past to an outward-looking policy. There is nothing like a crisis to concentrate the mind—it provided an urgency to revamp the Indian economic architecture. It should not mean concealing politically difficult decisions.

Endnotes

1. toppr. n.d. "Indian Economy (1950–1990)." https://www.toppr.com/guides/economics/indian-economy-1950-1990/industrial-policy/, (accessed April 27, 2019).
2. Indiabefore91.in. n.d. "License Raj." http://indiabefore91.in/license-raj, (accessed April 27, 2019).

CHAPTER 11

Economic Reforms in India

This chapter explains the concept, nature, need, and objectives of economic reforms in India. In any discussion on economic reforms, there ought to be three strands: (i) Why were reforms necessary and what was wrong with the earlier system? (ii) What reforms have been introduced? (iii) What remains to be done?

States do not function in a vacuum, but in specific social and political settings. The state (i.e., the government) does things that it should not and does not do things that it should. It is given "The Indian state has systematically underestimated the prevalence and the cost of "government failure." It often intervenes, arbitrarily or to correct supposed market failures, without any clear evidence that the market is failing, and so ends up damaging resource allocation and stifling business drive. At the same time, the Indian state does not deliver in the areas that fall squarely in its province, such as administering law and order, ensuring macroeconomic stability, delivering speedy justice, making sure that public services are provided, and creating an effective and adequate safety net for poor people. Both the state and the state–market relationship need urgent reform, which is no easy task in the context of India's political economy, with its democratic turbulence and powerful vested interests" (Joshi 2016).

The concept: The New Economic Policy (also known as economic reforms) is a set of policies and administrative procedures introduced in July 1991 to *bring about changes in the economic direction of the country*. It has two major components: *stabilization and structural reforms*.

The *stabilization* part has three components:

I. Management of balance of payments
II. Control of inflation
III. Fiscal correction

The structural reforms part has seven components:

    I. Exchange rate adjustment
    II. Liberalization of imports
  III. Rationalization of tariff structure
  IV. Delicensing/removal of licensing restrictions
    V. Financial sector reforms
  VI. Disinvestments of public sector shares
 VII. Foreign direct investment

It must be noted that while the *stabilization policies* were intended to correct the lapses and put the house in order in the short term, *the structural reform* was intended to accelerate economic growth over the medium term. Structural reform policies cannot succeed unless a degree of stabilization has been brought about. But stabilization by itself will not be adequate unless structural reforms are undertaken to avoid the recurrence of the problems. Structural reforms were broadly in the areas of industrial licensing and regulation, foreign trade and investment, and the financial sector. In relation to foreign trade policy, the aim was to liberalize the regime with respect to imports and try to bring about a closer link between exports and imports. Yet another objective was to reduce the tariff rates.

Implications of reforms: The three pronged approach has major implications for the functioning of the economy and its future direction. They imply a complete and a sudden break from the past, and several issues arise related to the following:

A) The *desirability of the pattern* of development sought
B) The *timing of the various policies,* and more importantly, their sequencing (and in fact the wisdom of the frequent changes in policy that has the effect of creating uncertainties in the Indian economy)
C) The relative importance attached to the different aspects of policy, in as much as domestic *priorities related to the* provision of education, health, and employment; globalization of the economy
D) The likely impact *of the package of policies*

In the wake of economic reforms the following three terms are frequently used: *deregulation, privatization, globalization*

A) *Deregulation* describes the process of removing rules imposed by the government that limit the economic freedom of individuals.
B) *Privatization* means removing the state and its agents from economic activities and letting these be undertaken by private individuals.
C) *Globalization,* however, has a much broader range; indeed, it has become a buzzword for many different phenomena. A comprehensive definition would define *globalization as the process of increasing both the scope and the actual incidence of interaction between people from all parts of the globe.*

Objectives: Economic reforms were intended to enable Indian industry to develop an outward orientation, and to allow freer play to market forces. Indian industry was to become more competitive, acquire modern and up-to-date technologies so that costs could be controlled and quality improved, establish production capacities that would allow cost advantages, become export oriented, and through investments by international companies tie in with the growing intra-firm trade of multinational companies. Reforms intended to achieve the following:

I. *Stabilization and macroeconomic balance* through fiscal, monetary, and exchange rate policies
II. *A liberalized trade regime with no import* licensing and tariff rates comparable to that of other industrializing developing countries
III. An *exchange rate system* that makes the rupee convertible, at least for current account transactions of the balance of payments
IV. A *competitive financial system* with sound regulations
V. An *industrial sector free of many controls*
VI. An *autonomous, competitive, and streamlined* public enterprise sector

There is a common thread running through all these measures. The objective is simple: *to improve the efficiency of the system.* The regulation mechanism involving a multitude of controls has fragmented capacity and reduced competition even in the public sector. The thrust of the economic reforms is toward *creating a more competitive environment in the economy as a* means to improving the productivity and efficiency of the system. This is to be achieved by removing the barriers to entry and the restrictions on the growth of firms.

The policy of economic reforms placed overwhelming reliance on private initiative and enterprise to achieve objectives. Public investment expenditures would over time play a secondary role. There are essentially two aspects to economic reform: *internal and external economic policies*. Each, in turn, has two aspects. In internal policymaking, one aspect is *debureaucratization and easing of controls*; the other pertains to *privatization of public enterprises*, following the neoliberal philosophy of laissez-faire and reliance on the market for all investment decisions, with minimum government intervention in the economy. Though these policies and procedures have a macroeconomic thrust, their impact on micro-level economic activities cannot be ignored. From this point of view the New Economic Policy will have its repercussions on the entire gamut of economic development.

A) *Market orientation*: The economic reform seeks to allocate the resources on the basis of the market forces of demand and supply. The government relaxed most of the regulations and controls to promote competition. The measures initiated to provide market orientation to the economy included delicensing, deregulation, disinvestment, dereservation of the industries exclusively reserved for the public sector, and liberalization of the foreign trade and investment policy.

B) *Selective government intervention*: The scope of government intervention was largely confined to the socially relevant areas. The government strengthened the institutional mechanism to facilitate functioning of markets. The government provided various inducements to the private sector to align its objectives with the national objectives through various economic policy measures like tax rebates, subsidies.

C) *Indicative planning*: The government replaced directive planning with indicative planning in the Eighth Plan (1992 to 1997). Under indicative planning there is no element of compulsion; the government uses persuasive economic policy measures to influence the activities of the private sector. The government pursues market-friendly policies for the mobilization and allocation of resources.

Problems faced by the economy prior to economic reforms: Before considering the various steps for restructuring the economy, it is important to be clear as to what were the most serious problems facing the Indian economy in 1990. Consider the following:

I. A large *fiscal deficit*, the underlying cause of which is *expenditure outpacing revenues*

II. A huge *foreign debt*, with a high debt-service ratio, and debt-exports ratio, which caused a downgrading of the country's credit rating and serious repayment problems

III. *Low levels of efficiency economy wide*, which resulted in a huge wastage of resources

IV. More contemporaneously, *a recessionary situation in the industrial sector*, stagnant agricultural output, and poor growth prospects in the economy as a whole, coupled with a *serious inflationary problem*

The situation that the nation and the economy had to face in mid-1991 was grim. The BoP situation had deteriorated so sharply and the foreign exchange reserves had fallen so low that the possibility of default in payment was imminent. On the domestic side, while the Indian economy had done extremely well in terms of real growth between 1985 and 1990, the fiscal situation had deteriorated sharply. The *budget deficit* as well as the overall *fiscal deficit* had sharply increased contributing on the one hand to a large increase in money supply and on the other to a sharp increase in interest payments. The country thus entered the 1990s with a fiscal deficit that was simply unsustainable.

Need for economic reform: The reforms were imperative for the following reasons:

I. The *downgrading of India's* credit rating made commercial loans difficult.

II. *Funds flow from West Asia dried up* following the Kuwait crisis, there were large withdrawals of NRI deposits during the early part of 1991, and foreign direct investment was low.
Aid for poorer countries was getting scarce because of larger claims by the former Soviet states and increased demands in the United

States for domestic spending. Compulsions of efficient use of aid made the case for reforms stronger.

III. Following the collapse of old attitudes worldwide and the emergence of a global market, India had no other alternative *but to initiate economic policy reforms.*

IV. However, reforms cannot be wholly attributed to these economic compulsions. The necessity for macroeconomic reforms had been steadily gaining credence in the 1980s. *The control system under the "permit raj"* had become unpopular. The timing was, therefore, ripe for an assault on the system and would be greeted with a sense of relief.

It is well known that structural adjustment involves *hard choices.* The choices are described as being hard because they often have implications that find disfavor with the populace at large, at least in the short run.

The evolution of the process of economic reforms: Though the process of relaxation of regulation of industry began in the early 1970s and of trade in the late 1970s, the pace of reform picked up significantly only in 1985. Major changes were announced between 1985 and 1988 with the process continuing to move forward thereafter. Indeed, during this latter period, liberalization had begun to take a somewhat activist form. In turn, GDP growth and the external sector registered a dramatic improvement in performance. The substantial yet half-hearted reforms of the 1980s gave way to the more systematic and deeper reforms of the 1990s and beyond. *This time around, there was a fundamental change in approach.* Until 1991, restrictions were the rule and reforms constituted their selective removal according to a "positive list" approach. But starting with the July 1991 package, absence of restrictions became the rule with a "negative list" approach taken to their retention. While the move toward this new regime has been decidedly gradual, with the process still far from complete, *the shift in the philosophy is beyond doubt.*

The economic reforms package: It is important to understand clearly what the economic reforms package is and equally important what it is not. Economic reforms can be briefly summed up as a package consisting of three separate sets of policies:

I. The *stabilization of the economy*, meaning thereby, the bringing into balance the aggregate demand and supply; the imbalance was in the main caused by large and endemic deficits in the Central Government's budget during the 1980s, which got reflected in the spiral of inflation at home and deficit in external payments abroad. The policies adopted in this context relate to budgetary and credit policies.

II. A *restructuring* of the Indian economy with a view to making Indian industry internationally competitive. The policies adopted in this context range from industrial and foreign trade policies to issues like the lending policies of financial institutions (including banks), the pattern of government expenditure and public investment, including the policy related to the public sector, and the approach on sick units and with regard to *subsidies generally and the subsidization of small business and farms in particular.*

III. *The globalization of the Indian economy*, throwing open (in stages) the import of all commodities (including consumer goods), reducing the customs tariffs, allowing free inflow of foreign capital (including short-term capital), opening up the service sector to foreign capital (especially in the matter of banking, insurance and shipping) and full convertibility of the rupee.

Thematically, the ingredients of the reform process are the following:

I. Eliminating quantitative restrictions on exports and imports

II. Bringing down and rationalizing tariffs, eliminating export subsidies, so that trade policy is neutral and equates the effective exchange rate for exports to the effective exchange rate for imports

III. Eliminating overvaluation in exchange rates and making the exchange rate market determined

IV. Reforming the public sector through disinvestments or through leasing and management contracts; in any case, eliminate public sector monopolies and introduce greater competition

V. Reforming monetary policy and transit to market-determined interest rates; reform the financial sector

VI. Bringing down budgetary deficits, target government subsidies better, and reform the tax structure so that indirect taxes become more transparent; simultaneously, bring down rates of direct taxation, while broadening the base

VII. In industry, removing barriers to entry and exit

VIII. Reforming the agricultural sector by making output and input prices market determined

IX. Targeting government expenditure on primary health, primary education, and the development of infrastructure; introduce social safety nets as protection against the effects of structural adjustments

Operation of economic reform: In a single stroke, the "Statement of Industrial Policy" dated July 24, 1991, changed the entire policy scenario:

I. *Did away with investment licensing* and myriad entry restriction on monopolistic and restrictive trade practices (MRTP) firms

II. Ended *public sector monopoly* in many sectors, and today, only railway transportation and atomic energy remain on it

III. Initiated a policy of automatic approval for foreign direct investment (FDI) up to 51 percent. The automatic approval of FDI up to 100 percent is given for all manufacturing activities in Special Economic Zones (SEZs) except those subject to licensing or public sector monopoly. Subject to licensing, defense is now open to private sector for 100 percent investment with FDI (also subject to licensing) up to 26 percent permitted.

IV. The *policy of continuity with change*, trimmed the licensing to only five sectors with all of them having justification on health, safety, or environmental grounds: (a) arms and ammunition, explosives and allied items of defense equipment, defense aircraft and warships; (b) atomic substances; (c) narcotics and psychotropic substances and hazardous chemicals; (d) distillation and brewing of alcoholic drinks; and (e) cigarettes/cigars and manufactured tobacco substitutes.

V. Did away with entry restrictions on MRTP firms. Again, the policy was notable for its unequivocal renunciation of the past approach: The MRTP Act 1969, has been repealed. The provisions related to merger, amalgamation, and takeover have been repealed. Similarly, the provisions regarding restrictions on acquisition of and transfer of shares will be appropriately incorporated in the Companies Act,1956. These changes are now in place.

External trade: The July 1991 package also made a break from the 1980s approach of selective liberalization on the external trade front by replacing the positive list approach of listing license-free items on the open general license (OGL) list with a negative list approach. It also addressed tariff reform in a more systematic manner rather than relying on selective exemptions on statutory tariffs. In subsequent years, liberalization has been extended to trade in services as well.

Merchandise trade liberalization: The July 1991 reforms did away with import licensing on virtually all intermediate inputs and capital goods. Today, except for a handful of goods disallowed on environmental, health, and safety grounds and a few others that are canalized, such as fertilizer, cereals, edible oils, and petroleum products, all goods can be imported without a license or other restrictions.

A major task of the reforms in the 1990s and beyond has been to *lower tariffs*. This has been done in a gradual fashion by compressing the top tariff rate while rationalizing the tariff structure through a reduction in the number of tariff bands. The 1990s reforms were also accompanied by the lifting of *exchange controls* that had served as an extra layer of restrictions on imports. As a part of the 1991 reform, the government *devalued* the rupee by 22 percent against the dollar from Rs. 21.2 to Rs. 25.8 per dollar. In February 1992, a *dual exchange rate system* was introduced, which allowed exporters to sell 60 percent of their foreign exchange in the free market at higher price and 40 percent to the government at the lower official price. Importers were authorized to purchase foreign exchange in the open market at the higher price, effectively ending the exchange control. Within a year of establishing this market exchange rate, the official exchange rate was unified with it. Starting in February 1994, many current account transactions, including all current business transactions, education, medical expenses, and foreign travel, were also permitted at the market exchange rate. These steps culminated in *India accepting the IMF Article VIII obligations, which made the rupee officially convertible on the current account.*

Liberalization of trade in services: Since 1991, India has also carried out a substantial liberalization of *trade in services*. Traditionally, services sectors have been subject to heavy government intervention. Public sector presence has been conspicuous in the key sectors of insurance, banking, and telecommunications. Nevertheless, considerable progress has been made toward opening the door wider to private sector participation, including foreign investors, in them.

Until recently, *insurance* was a state monopoly. On December 7, 1999, the Indian parliament passed the *Insurance Regulatory and Development Authority (IRDA)* Bill, which established an Insurance Regulatory and Development Authority and opened the door to private entry, including foreign investors. Though the public sector dominates in the banking sector, private banks are permitted to operate in it. In addition, *foreign banks* are allowed to open a specified number of new branches every year.

The telecommunications sector has experienced much greater opening to the private sector, including foreign investors. Until the early 1990s, the sector was a state monopoly. The 1994 National Telecommunications Policy provided for opening cellular as well as basic and value-added telephone services to the private sector, with foreign investors granted entry. Rapid changes in technology led to the adoption of the New Telecom Policy in 1999, which provides the current policy framework.

The infrastructure sector has also been opened to foreign investment. FDI up to 100 percent under automatic route is permitted in projects for the construction and maintenance of *roads, highways, vehicular bridges, toll roads, vehicular tunnels, ports, and harbors*. In the construction and maintenance of ports and harbors, automatic approval for foreign equity up to 100 percent is available. *Only railways remain off limits to private entry.* Since 1991, several attempts have been made to bring the private sector, including FDI, into the *power sector* but without perceptible success.

Impact of economic reforms: Trade liberalization had a much more visible effect on external trade in the 1990s than in the 1980s. Liberalization also had a significant effect on growth in some of the key services sectors. This growth was mostly due to the fast growth in communication services, financial services, business services, and community services. The most disappointing aspect of the 1990s experience, however, has been a *lack of acceleration of growth in the industrial sector*. This is largely due to labor laws; industry in India is increasingly outsourcing its activities so that growth in industry is actually being counted in terms of growth in services.

Investment into industry, whether domestic or foreign, has been sluggish. Foreign investors have been hesitant to invest in the industry for much the same reasons as the domestic investors. At the same time, the capacity of the formal services sector to absorb foreign investment is limited. The information technology sector has shown promise but its base is still small. Moreover, this sector is more intensive in skilled labor than physical capital. Therefore, the solution to both trade and FDI expansion in India lies in stimulating growth in industry.

Labor issues lie at the heart of the success or failure of a structural adjustment program. The final impact on people in general and the poor in particular is the real yardstick by which the success of an adjustment program should be judged. The impact of the ongoing reforms on individuals, poverty, and income distribution continues to be the source of much controversy; a particular matter of concern is whether the poor bear a disproportionate share of the burden of the cost of adjustment, especially in the short run.

The *absence of an exit policy* for labor is the ostensible reason for the reluctance of some foreign investors to enter India. The economic reforms undertaken so far have attempted to usher in an era of high growth, with the underlying assumption that such growth would necessarily filter down, thereby enhancing economic welfare across the board. The assumption of effective percolation has been guided by the further presumption of existence of strong forward and backward linkages.

Globalization is centered on the integration of international markets for *goods, services, technology, finance, and labor*. It is underpinned by the opening up of national economies to global market forces and a corresponding reduction in the scope of the state to shape national macroeconomic policies. Indeed, the end of geography symbolizes the thrust of globalization with far-reaching implications for regional, national, and local economies. In this respect, globalization is expected to unfold through trade and finance with profound consequences for the structure of BoP, investment, growth, income distribution, employment, and poverty. However, the nature of interaction between the new phenomenon and economies (at the different levels) poses critical questions for the prosperity or the *marginalization of developing countries and their poor*. In this frame, a critical analytical issue is the extent to which globalization will undermine the state and its capacity to formulate macroeconomic policies.

Problems associated with economic reform: A market economy with information deficiencies and inadequate institutions hurts both the consumers and the state. It can lead to serious sociopolitical fallouts (Smith 2016). Only in crisis times does the polity reform, but then there are endemic problems to make reforms a constantly recurring topic. Reforms are always partial as political courage is in limited supply. In India's peculiar electoral cycle, where every 6 months there is an election somewhere, the central leadership loses heart with the first reversal in a state election, no matter how small the state. The courage to face unpopularity and think in five-year cycles is rare. But reform and restructuring are constantly required in any economy, let alone India, which is far short of realizing its potential.

The ground situation is abysmal in terms of malnutrition, open defecation, waste management, stagnation in manufacturing, and continual crisis in farming, where four-fifths of farms are unsustainable in terms of affording their owners a decent livelihood.

The public sector gets too much mollycoddling, nonperforming loans of a grossly inefficient public sector undertaking (PSU) banking sector, all these stand witness to the root of India's problems, but will not be reformed any time soon.

The state has weak competence. Despite that, governments of all political persuasion load it with more tasks—new entitlements (food security while public distribution system (PDS) shops constantly fail), environmental regulations (without correcting chronic underpricing of water, power, and public land), and additional rewards and perks (without improving incentive structures or efficiency enhancing arrangements). Nothing is removed as having lost utility—only left as a continuing expense while more is added. The state cannot deliver good quality education at any level—primary, secondary, or tertiary. The consumers go away to private providers if they can afford or molder in colleges where they are barely functionally literate after 3 years. There is not much hope that the state will be reformed any time soon. The bureaucracy may not see the need for any urgent reforms. It is the politician who has to raise the standard of reforms. It would need a horrendous crisis, of a magnitude one would not wish, before Indian politics changes its ways (Desai 2016).

To ensure permanent change will require deeper reforms, however. If wholesale ministerial corruption is reportedly much reduced, there is still little clarity over how political parties are financed. Making India less bureaucratic would also be a boon. A certain brand of tycoon has thrived because getting things done often requires sharp elbows and sharper business practices. Magnates who are politically astute will still have an edge if knowing how to dodge a price cap imposed on a ministerial whim, for example, is a surer guide to success than knowing how to run a factory. Such shenanigans have not stopped. A decent financial system is the best defense against cronyism.[1]

Endnote

1. The Economist. April 19, 2018. "The Humbling of India's Tycoons." https://www.economist.com/leaders/2018/04/21/the-humbling-of-indias-tycoons, (accessed July 17, 2019).

CHAPTER 12

The Present State of the Indian Economy and the Task Ahead

Development is a challenge globally, not just in India. It is India's 73rd year of independence (1947 to 2019). In this chapter an effort will be made to take a look at the current state of the Indian economy and its future direction. India may be the 5th largest economy in total income, but it is 145th in terms of per capita income. The vision has to be that India will be in the top 100, if not top 50.

In 2018, India's per capita GDP was $2,015.60 and this makes sense as the economy is currently sized at $2.7 trillion, and the population is around 1.35 billion. "In purchasing power parity (PPP) terms, India is the third largest economy already, only next to China and the United States. India's PPP per capita GDP (measured in 2011 dollars) rose to $6,899 in 2018 from $1,886 in 1991, when economic reforms began. Many economists believe PPP is a better gauge of an economy's strength" (Kalbag 2019) while making international comparison.

The slowdown of the growth rate began in 2012, reversed in 2015, but over the last 2 years it has slowed again. The last official quarterly growth data, pertaining to the first quarter of 2019, shows GDP growth to be at 5.8 percent. Turning to other micro data, India's automobile sector is stalling, and the balance sheets of Indian corporations have worsened. Companies' combined borrowings were up 13.2 percent in FY19 but their net worth did not rise comparably. The Indian economy's slowdown is accompanied by a high unemployment rate across the labor force—skilled, semiskilled, and unskilled. The major contributing factor for the slowdown from the demand side is a deceleration in investment rate measured in terms of the percentage share of gross fixed capital formation (GFCF) to GDP. When analyzed from the supply or economic activity side, technically called gross value added (GVA), the economic growth slowdown was primarily attributed to the collapse of agricultural growth. There has been consistent deceleration in agriculture and allied sectors.

At the moment, unemployment is the biggest challenge. Nearly 20 million youth are ready to enter the workforce every year in India. To address this influx to the workforce, the country needs to create nearly 55,000 jobs every day for the foreseeable future. That is a daunting, but not impossible task. To create jobs on that scale, the economy will need to grow by double digits.

The primary sector takes up over half the total workforce. Interestingly, this is followed by the tertiary sector, which takes up a little over a quarter of the remaining, followed finally by the secondary sector. Although India ranks second in worldwide farm output, it lags behind in crop yield per unit area of farms. Although India is a huge producer of minerals and chemicals, domestic demand is so high that India still has to import a lot. The tertiary sector produces the largest share of the nation's GDP. It includes the IT sector, transportation, tourism, banking, finance, and energy among other fields. The nation's IT sector has seen rapid expansion, with seven Indian firms being listed in the world's top 15 technology outsourcing companies. The expansion is attributed to skilled workers who demand low wages.

India is a large market for travel and tourism. It is the third largest in the world. As of 2017 to 2018, 81.1 million people were employed in the tourism sector, which was 12.38 percent of total employment in the country. The government has set a target of 20 million foreign tourist arrivals (FTAs) by 2020 and double the foreign exchange earnings as well.[1]

India has made more progress against poverty in the quarter century and change since liberalization started widening the scope of citizens' economic choices than in all the prior decades. By 2022, the number of Indians living in extreme poverty is expected to drop to 20 million.[2] This is startling progress seeing where India stood at the turn of the century. India has made appreciable progress on some fronts—from the government vacating space for the private sector in various industries to monetary policy, with the Reserve Bank of India (RBI) adopting an inflation-targeting regime in 2015.

The economy is constrained by a set of challenging external and internal conditions. Externally, global economic expansion and trade growth have both been slowing, since 2017 and the risk of that downward slide being accelerated by some catastrophic global event has risen exponentially since the beginning of 2019 (Mundle 2019). The withdrawal of the generalized system of preferences (GSP) by the United States comes as an additional setback. This will put pressure on the exchange rate and make the management of capital flows and financing of the current account deficit (CAD) in a nondisruptive manner difficult.

The internal situation is equally grim. Macroeconomic indicators, hitherto conflicting, are all now consistently reflecting a severe growth slowdown. Growth of GDP, agriculture, industry, investment, and trade has declined in real terms. Growth of private consumption remains high, but that too is beginning to slow down. Meanwhile, the Periodic Labor Force Survey results have confirmed the high unemployment, while severe distress seems to have become the new normal for rural India.

For the first time in 6 years, foreign direct investment (FDI) equity inflows dropped 1 percent, year-on-year, to $44.4 billion, in FY19, which could put pressure on the country's BoP. The top three sectors that received the highest equity inflows were services, computer hardware and software, and trading. These accounted for 45 percent of total equity inflows in FY19. Inflows in services sector grew 37 percent in FY19 to $9.2 billion. Equity inflows in the automobile sector witnessed a growth of 26 percent. In contrast, equity inflows contracted 5 percent in the telecom sector.[3]

According to the Centre for Monitoring Indian Economy (CMIE), the monetary value of stalled projects touched Rs. 2.68 trillion by the end of March 2019,[4] the highest value since CMIE began compiling data in 1995. While this also includes private projects, reviving stalled government projects alone has the potential to jump-start the economy. There will, of course, be the usual lament about rising fiscal deficits and high government borrowings crowding out private borrowing. The stalling rate is calculated as a percentage of the total projects under implementation so that the values are comparable across time. The stalling rate of private sector projects, which has hovered above 20 percent since the September 2017 quarter, reached 26.1 percent in the June 2019 quarter. Within sectors, the manufacturing and power sectors have suffered the most with stalling rates of 27.2 percent and 20.4 percent, respectively. They, along with the service sector, contribute to 92 percent of the total stalled projects (Alexander 2019).

Lack of funds remains the most important reason for stalled projects in recent quarters, implying a liquidity crunch as underfinanced banks and stressed corporations are finding it increasingly difficult to finance their projects. Other major bottlenecks include problems with fuel and raw materials and delays in land acquisition. Investors' appetite may also have been affected by the economy-wide slowdown.

The government's current expenditure is focused on pump-priming the economy and boosting aggregate demand. This has been achieved partly through a heavy emphasis on welfare payments and social sector resource transfers, streaking the government's economic policy with a social democratic tint. But policy now needs an urgent pivot toward facilitating more investment. On the demand side, the only functioning engine of growth seems to be private consumption. With a substantial cut in capital expenditure by the government to conform to the fiscal deficit target and with private investment not picking up, capital formation too is showing deceleration. Exports also have been stagnant. The twin balance sheet problem is still a major factor.

The competence of the state has declined in relation to the increased demands on it, manifested, for example, in the dire condition of the provisioning of public goods such as education and health care. First, there is a glaring "administrative deficit" that needs to be corrected. Second, money and crime have taken over politics to a growing extent. Corruption in public life has increased manifold; the prediction of some analysts that it would abate as a result of the 1991 reforms is now seen to be hopelessly optimistic. "Ordinary citizens find that back-handers to police and government officials are necessary to get even the simplest things done" (Joshi 2016). The symbiosis between the economic, political, and bureaucratic elite evolved over the years into a polished system of crony capitalism. This has eroded the popular legitimacy of India's post-1991 move to a more free market economy.

The Task Ahead

It is argued that the "partial reforms model" since 1991 has now run into diminishing returns. The next round of radical reforms is needed to boost growth; in Joshi's (2016) words, "to keep the engine of productivity firing on all cylinders." The key political economy challenge is to establish the correct balance between the state, the market, and the private sector. India has yet to complete the move to becoming a modern social democracy. Joshi recommends a five-pronged agenda—privatization, employment creation, deep fiscal adjustment, primary education, and building state capacity. There is little to disagree with in this broad wish list.[5] There are many policy paradoxes that can be gleaned from Joshi's (2018) lecture:

I. Are banks a special case that need to be kept outside the ambit of aggressive privatization?

II. Do wage subsidies have a role to play in promoting employment growth by organized industry?

III. Can a negotiated deal with the trade unions reduce some of their opposition to labor market reforms?

IV. Is it possible to promote labor-intensive exports when the real effective exchange rate is appreciating?

V. How can India have a deep fiscal adjustment by slashing nonmerit subsidies as well as minimizing dysfunctional tax exemptions?

VI. Can these fiscal gains be used to build infrastructure and fund a program for universal basic income?

VII. How can one get the Indian state to do less and do more at the same time?

The past few years have seen important changes such as macroeconomic stability, a new monetary policy framework, the GST, and the bankruptcy law. The goal of inclusive growth in terms of job creation in the organized sector remains elusive. Structured thinking on India's economic transformation is still needed. Broadly, if India can get the 5Ds (democracy, demography, disruption, disintermediation, and distribution) right, it would have secured the legacy of the country and realized the promise and potential the founding fathers saw for independent

India. India is on a cusp—the future looks bright, but subject to the country managing the 5Ds (Padmanabhan 2016).

To be assured of good times to come, structural and institutional changes are essential. The manner in which the state functions, the behavior of market participants, and the framework of the relationship between state and market in India need to change. And they need to change in a fundamental manner. That change should be initiated now when public opinion is demanding it and not later when entrenched interests assert themselves (Reddy 2017a). The argument is that with "business-as-usual" policies, India will be hard put to achieve the high-quality and enduring per capita growth that would be necessary for it to become a prosperous nation in the next quarter century (Joshi 2016). The central government with a fresh mandate is expected to pursue a bold agenda. Political power is no guarantee of success in economic policy. Improving the material well-being of India's long-suffering masses will require focused attention to the nation's economic challenges (Singh 2019b). The frame of the economic policy decisions of the government is expected to cover the various sectors of the economy having the following pattern:

Growth rate: The Economic Survey (2018 to 2020) drew a pragmatic blueprint for the next 5 years. To achieve the objective of becoming a $5 trillion economy by 2024 to 2025, India needs to sustain a real GDP growth rate of 8 percent. International experience, especially from high-growth East Asian economies, suggests that such growth can only be sustained by a "virtuous cycle" of savings, investment, and exports catalyzed and supported by a favorable demographic phase. A big roadblock to achieving double-digit growth, however, is India's poor infrastructure, which is not where it should be. Almost certainly, India will be dependent on foreign investors for infrastructure money. But to attract investments at such a large scale, the government should tick all the remaining boxes in the reform to-do lists. India needs public investment or government expenditure to foster growth impulses in the economy.

Employment: The unemployment problem in India arises not out of lack of job opportunities, but due to the lack of skill of laborers. Training them will lead to faster industrialization and will increase the number of goods produced by the manufacturing sector. When it comes to the creation of jobs, economic "growth" does not necessarily translate into corresponding, or even adequate, employment opportunities. The government needs to urgently look at creating or enabling new employment opportunities. This ties into investments in physical and social infrastructure and increasing efficiency through higher productivity. "The *Make in India* project demands a huge number of skilled labor in India. According to India Skills Report, just 34 per cent were found employable out of about 1,00,000 candidates" (Chandar 2016). The need to create jobs, Make in India, Stand-Up India, Start-Up India, and so on hope to create more jobs and enterprises for India's burgeoning youth population. The problem is that the rapid advance of automation is expected to reduce jobs in manufacturing and even services (Maira 2017). The definition of jobs full time, formal sector jobs, or livelihoods (Remember the *pakodawala?*) needs to be delved into (a person who sells an Indian dish consisting of pieces of vegetable, chicken, etc., dipped in a spiced batter and deep-fried: served with a piquant sauce. The term was used in the context of employment generation in the informal sector. *Pakodawala is a self-employed person).* It may need anthropologists as well as statisticians to understand what has been happening in the economy. Now, is the time to face up to these issues and fix the system. That would solve a long-term problem (Desai 2019a).

The economy's animal spirits—increasing investment: Through the mantra of "investment-led growth," the "Economic Survey" (2018 to 2020) puts the highest priority on strengthening the supply side to rev up economic activity. Besides infrastructure, the other key areas where the government needs to multiply investments are education and health care. In order to develop a highly skilled workforce, public spending on basic, vocational, and technical education is an absolute necessity. Just as with education, the government must have a big vision and a large-scale program for health care. From preventive and prenatal care to greater access to health care in the rural areas, the challenges are many. The Ayushman Bharat Yojana scheme is expected to help as many as 500 million people. It is a great first step. In addressing health care challenges, there is a need to enlist a huge pool of physicians of Indian origin around the globe who are willing, ready, and available to help.

The "Economic Survey" (2018 to 2020) nicely lays out the direction with a focus on private investment and export-led growth. It shows how investment, exports, productivity, employment, and competitiveness are interlinked to create a "virtuous" cycle of growth. In a virtuous cycle, "investment, productivity growth, job creation, demand and exports feed into each other and enable animal spirits in the economy to thrive". But the key driver for it is investment—more specifically, private investment. The "Economic Survey" is right that the macroeconomic stability indicators—whether pertaining to inflation, external current account, or even fiscal balances—are much better than they were 5 years ago and it is time to "shift gears" to enable an average annual real GDP growth of 8 percent for India to become a $5 trillion economy by 2024 to 2025.

A necessary condition for reviving investment is lowering the cost of money. The Monetary Policy Committee is moving the needle in the right direction. But lowering the policy rate alone will not transmit to lower interest rates in a world of fiscal dominance. Furthermore, to effectively revive the credit cycle and the investment cycle, measures will have to be combined with sustained efforts to push the bankruptcy resolution process to clean up the nonperforming loans overhang for banks, and also resolve the crisis now being faced by nonbanking financial companies (NBFCs). This appears to be a tall order.

Agricultural sector: The Indian economy needs to modernize. Modernizing agriculture will lead to more yield of crop per unit area, increasing the share of agriculture and other primary sector activities' share of GDP in India. Expansion of agricultural activities will lead to a chain increase of agro-based industries. Modernization will also lead to increased income for families in rural areas, thus increasing their purchasing power, which in turn expands the existing market for manufactured goods, and expansion of the economy. Poverty alleviation should be given the highest priority. If India seeks to eradicate poverty and the poor state of farmers in India, it must convert unskilled laborers to skilled laborers and tutor farmers about modern techniques of farming.

"Distorting policies, such as enforcing stock-holding limits and frequent export bans, should be corrected. Repeal of the Essential Commodities Act, 1955 and breaking the monopsony from Agricultural

Produce Marketing Committees are important too. In fact, a policy focus on enhancing investment in storage, processing, and marketing, and timely information on both input and output prices to the farmers through upscaled extension will help them to enhance their yield and get remunerative prices" (Rao 2019).

Manufacturing sector and Micro, Small and Medium Enterprises (MSMEs): Acceleration in growth of manufacturing requires changes in the investment climate. India needs a reindustrialization drive to create a level playing field for the country's private manufacturers and increase their R&D intensification. If the government wants to create more jobs and value addition at home, it must immediately formalize and implement the Defence Production Policy (DPP), which has some excellent ideas, such as "make India among the top-five countries in aerospace and defence industries," and leverage military and civil aviation for indigenization. It, however, calls for reducing imports. Defense production also needs to be prioritized over procurement. To come out of the morass of low-tech development, India must curtail imports and channel funds to proven private high-tech companies, fueling a takeoff and creating jobs and prosperity at home. It is high time the government forges a compact with the good, high-tech, proven companies in the Indian private sector and focus on domestic high-tech industrial promotion and job creation (Purushottam 2019).

The travails of an informal enterprise that seeks to formalize should not take much time and effort. There is a need for root and branch evaluation of the policies, rules, and regulations governing small enterprises. As the "Economic Survey" (2018 to 2020) suggests, large firms should work in an interlinked way with their MSMEs, not one against the other. "Small enterprises must grow in both rural and urban India to support the large factories that will themselves become more automated and employ less people. Moreover, such small enterprises will provide the steps needed for people to earn and learn" (Maira 2017).

Fiscal policy: There are many useful suggestions by the "Economic Survey" that may be worth considering. The first is a redesign of tax policy, including for start-ups. High tax rates on corporate profits and notices received by new economy companies on angel funding from venture capital investors are certainly not a good idea. They need a complete review, especially in the current context where animal spirits are low. Reviving those spirits will present the biggest and most immediate challenge for the government. It is important to recognize that a boost to public investment in infrastructure will have a large fiscal cost. It can restructure public expenditure to cut back at least a part of the nonmerit subsidies that add up to around 5.7 percent of the GDP. Tax concessions and exemptions that add up to another 5 percent of the GDP can also be pared. The question is whether the government will use its massive mandate to enforce such fiscal discipline (Mundle 2019).

The next challenge lies in the country's tax system. To reduce revenue deficit appropriate structural tax reforms by widening the tax base and increasing voluntary tax compliance—a long-term game—is needed. India remains an underperformer in terms of its tax-to-GDP ratio, adjusted for its per capita GDP. The goods and services tax (GST) needs to be tweaked, simplified, eased for taxpayers, and implemented fully. Simplification, and possibly even lowering of rates, can improve both compliance and enforcement. While local and other subnational taxes can often be inefficient, the central government should consider allowing local and even state governments to increase their tax authority, even by piggybacking income tax surcharges on central collections. Improving the assessment and collection of property taxes requires political will and administrative competence. Property taxes are relatively progressive and should be difficult to avoid. In any case, increasing public resources in ways that are nondistortionary and nonextortionate is an imperative. The need for these resources to clean up the financial sector mess adds to the urgency (Singh 2019b).

Disinvestment: One important window for increasing capital expenditure for the government is to activate strategic disinvestment. Any enterprise wasting taxpayer money should be sold off. This should be the next revolution in Indian economic policy. The government has to erase the ill effects of "old economics." But then the culture of reliance on public sector, government subsidies, and antigrowth legislation in land, labor, and commodity markets has to be repealed. The psychology of public good, private bad has to be altered (Desai 2019b). It took India 20 years after 1991 to accept FDI without reservations. But its benefits have been immense. The slimming down of the public sector must be the next transformation. It will generate resources to finance various measures of economic policy.

The NITI Aayog has done considerable work in identifying the companies for disinvestment, and the government should start the process by completely shedding Air India. Hopefully, it will muster the courage to overcome the stalling process by special interest groups. An active disinvestment process will buoy the markets and will make the process smoother. It must await its time, however, and can only be a slow process. What is needed is a credible philosophy of disinvestment, relating to strategic capability beyond private sector capacity and the desirability of state presence in some sectors. Unfortunately, this is a politically unpopular move in a democracy where secure government jobs are prized and there was no clearly enunciated philosophy about disinvestment. Investors need to be informed about a philosophy of disinvestment. While the government will certainly disinvest in some loss-making units, it clearly does not intend to privatize companies that are core to its welfarist strategies, including banks.

Financial system: The foremost challenge is fixing the country's financial sector, especially its banks. The overhang of debts that are on the balance sheets of banks and other financial institutions, but will almost certainly never be repaid, prevents new investment taking place to the degree it needs to. The new bankruptcy law, and the RBI's attempt to make it operational and effective, has run into obstacles, which, if not removed, will allow the situation to linger and even worsen, rather than the hoped for improvement. In that case ranking in the World Bank's Ease of Doing Business measure will be meaningless. Whether additional new laws or new regulations are needed is up to the experts, but there has to be political will to move quickly through a process that will inevitably be painful (Singh 2019b).

Businesses need capital that they acquire from financial markets. This requires a healthy credit culture wherein debts are repaid, insolvencies are dealt with in a quick and orderly way, and banks are free to lend to the most productive borrower. More generally, private businesses, locally and globally, need to feel that India is business friendly—its industrial and trade policies are not subject to sudden reversals, enforcement agencies are independent, public data is reliable, and the country values domain specialists in overseeing its market infrastructure. This is about generating confidence in India's institutional structure to encourage greater investment and newer technology inflows through FDI.

External sector: Regarding exports, the discretionary tampering with tariff rates in recent years, which destroyed the gains of a quarter century of trade reforms, will have to be reversed, along with an active exchange rate policy to prevent an appreciation of the real effective exchange rate. These economic policy measures will have to be backed by visible improvements in logistics and communications to level the playing field for Indian exporters (Mundle 2019).

Labor laws: Sequencing reforms is critical, and labor reforms can only be instituted when unemployment rates are low and the economy can sustain a safety net or social security system for the unemployed. Labor laws in all advanced economies are backed by robust safety nets. This is the time to impart flexibility to the labor market to enhance labor-intensive industrialization and exports. Addressing these require reforms to India's existing land acquisition and labor policies. Current labor laws make large-scale hiring costly for firms.

Regulations and governance reforms: The major problem faced in the country is in the factor markets. It is time that the government come out with the law and regulations regarding land consolidation and leasing, to allow for nonexploitative contract farming. Similarly, land acquisition has been a major problem for expanding highways. Governance reform is as essential to India's growth as economic reforms over the next 5 years. Economic reforms with patchy implementation can create a regulatory maze. Badly designed regulations have proved counterproductive in many sectors. It was suggested that the top leadership should set a broad reform agenda and give autonomy to state and local bureaucrats to implement them on the basis of regional uniqueness. Between 2018 and 2019, Indian states were expected to spend 72 percent more than the central government. This means that the majority of public spending decisions are outside the purview of the central government[6] and central schemes, such as Swachh Bharat and Smart Cities Mission, also rely on actual implementation by state officials. The central government needs to play the role of an orchestra conductor to revive India's faltering economy. An efficient government—one that draws down its intervention where it is distortionary and goes big where it needs to—is a better goal.

Conclusion: There is no quick fix in the given situation. The government, therefore, needs to make bold structural reforms, engaging itself with supply-side management. The conventional demand management of lowering interest rate through policy repo rate reduction is only a second-best solution at the current juncture. But things are going to get worse before they get better. India has a problem of muddled thinking on economic policy. India needs very deep reforms and steady growth. India's economy requires skillful policy maneuvers. "What is needed is to cut the culture of permissionism. There is a reason governments allow this to persist" (Basu 2019). Retaining the same centralized decision-making model is an impediment to India's economic prospects.

The government should not be afraid of accommodating a slight slippage in the fiscal deficit target. There is nothing sacrosanct about 3.5 percent of GDP or a line in the sand. The boundaries were drawn in different times when circumstances were different. It's now time to think differently. In general, supply management in terms of enhancement of productivity holds the key to higher growth and employment. Bold policy decisions on land reforms, labor market reforms, tax reforms for voluntary compliance, skill development through vocational training, strengthening of physical and social infrastructure, and autonomy for key institutions should be the focus of the government. The RBI's mandate to control inflation must not get diluted. In general, it's important to restore the credibility of all independent institutions, the data-crunching agencies included. National statistics should be transparent and trustworthy. Yet, the more serious issue is not statistical but causal. Some of these are in the works.

With such an overwhelming mandate, the time is opportune to walk the talk of being a reformist government. Eventually, the masses will judge the policy through its effects on employment, prices, availability of output, and declining rate of inflation. That is why implementation of policy is more important. The science of optimal control in economic policy is a complex one. No government in the world has ever got everything right or disastrously wrong, for which we can all be only grateful (Desai 2019a).

Endnotes

1. IBEF. May, 2019. "Indian Tourism and Hospitality Industry Analysis." https://www.ibef.org/industry/indian-tourism-and-hospitality-industry-analysis-presentation, (accessed July 20, 2019).

2. Livemint. 2018. "Why Economic Freedom Is Important in India." https://www.livemint.com/Opinion/GwJsB1bcM5v2mbVNmBL7FK/Opinion—Why-economic-freedom-is-important-in-India.html, (accessed July 20, 2019).

3. Financial Express. June 29, 2019. "FDI Inflows Fall—Explained Through Graphics." https://www.financialexpress.com/opinion/fdi-inflows-fall-explained-through-graphics/1622568/, (accessed July 24, 2019).

4. CMIE. July 24, 2019. "Quarterly CapEx Aggregates." https://www.cmie.com/, (accessed July 24, 2019).

5. MINT. December 14, 2017. "India: The Road to Wider Prosperity." https://www.livemint.com/Opinion/kGgHFvI4q97xVPZT4BwbRN/India-the-road-to-wider-prosperity.html, (accessed July 24, 2019).

6. PRS. n.d. "State of State Finances: 2018-19." https://www.prsindia.org/policy/discussion-papers/state-state-finances-2018-19, (accessed July 24, 2019).

CHAPTER 13

Indian Economic Thought/Thinkers

This chapter will be devoted to a brief review of the development of Indian economic thought in ancient times. There are two important thinkers who contributed toward the economic thinking. They are Thiruvalluvar and Kautilya.

Thiruvalluvar (351 to 350 BC) is a fundamental thinker. Even though scholars differ widely over the estimation of the period of birth of Thiruvalluvar, it is generally believed that he belonged to the Sangam Age in Tamil Nadu around the 3rd century AD. Thiruvalluvar's work is marked by pragmatic idealism. A large part of Valluvar's economic ideas are found in the second part of *Thirukkural*, the *porutpal*. It deals with wealth.

Thirukkural, a book of ethics, is Thiruvalluvar's immortal work. Thiruvalluvar's *Thirukkural* throws light on the economic thought in ancient South India. A large part of his economic ideas are found in the second part of *Thirukkural*, the "'porutpal." It deals with wealth. Since rain provides food, it forms the basis for stable economic life. Agriculture, which is the most fundamental economic activity, depends on rain. "It is rain that both ruins and aids the ruined to rise." The following are the salient features of Thiruvalluvar's economic thinking:

I. *Factors of Production*: Thiruvalluvar has made many passing references about the factors of production, that is, Land, Labor, Capital, Organization, Time, Technology, and so on. He says, "Unfailing harvest, competent body of men, group of men, whose wealth knows no diminution, are the components of an economy."

II. *Agriculture*: Agriculture is the most fundamental economic activity. It is the axle-pin of the world, for on its prosperity revolves the prosperity of other sectors of the economy. "The ploughmen alone," he says, "live as the freemen of the soil; the rest are mere slaves that follow on their toil." Valluvar believed that agriculture was superior to all other occupations.

III. *Public Finance*: He elaborately explained Public Finance under the headings Public Revenue, Financial Administration, and Public Expenditure. He stated these as creation of revenue, collection of revenue, management of revenue, public expenditure. Valluvar recommended a balanced budget. "It is not a great misfortune for a state if its revenues are limited, provided the expenditure is kept within bounds." He has given certain guidelines for a budgetary policy. "Budget for a surplus, if possible, balances the budget at other times, but never budget for a deficit." He advocates *defense, public works, and social services* as the main items of public expenditure.

IV. *External Assistance*: He was against seeking external assistance. Countries taking external assistance are not to be considered as countries at all. In other words, he advocated a self-sufficient economy.

V. *Poverty and Begging*: Valluvar considered freedom from hunger as one of the fundamental freedoms that should be enjoyed by every citizen. Poverty is the root cause of all other evils, which would lead to everlasting sufferings.

VI. *Wealth*: He regarded wealth as only a means and not an end. He said, "Acquire a great fortune by noble and honorable means" and condemned hoarding and described hoarded wealth as profitless richness. To him industry was real wealth and labor the greatest resource.

VII. *Welfare State*: Thiruvalluvar stood for a welfare state. In a welfare state there will be no poverty, illiteracy, and disease. The important elements of a welfare state are perfect health of the people without disease, abundant wealth, good crop, prosperity and happiness, and full security for the people.[1]

Thiruvalluvar underscores the importance of wealth, which covers a broad spectrum of economic activities. These include aspects such as the pursuit of material well-being, keeping a balance between baser and otherworldly objectives, cognizance of charity as an instrument to address market failure, prudence in collection and use of taxes, bargaining, and *verna* (color or class) as a means of division of labor and distributive justice. (Deodhar 2018, p.15).

Kautilya's *Arthashastra* (c. 350 to 275 BCE): Thanawala (1997) has observed that the *Arthashastra* is not widely known among scholars outside India. The title of a session at the annual meeting of the History of Economics Society held during June 1994 was "Arthashastra: A Neglected Text from the 4th Century BC!" One should note that while Kautilya's work was not mentioned by Schumpeter in his authoritative *History of Economic Analysis* (Schumpeter 1954), Spengler wrote more than once at length about it (Spengler 1971, 1980). Kautilya's political thoughts are summarized in a book he wrote, known as the Arthashastra, a Sanskrit name that is translated as "The Science of Material Gain." This book was lost for many centuries and a copy of it written on palm leaves was rediscovered in India in 1904 CE. The *Arthashastra* is a handbook for running an empire effectively and contains detailed information about specific topics. Diplomacy and war are the two points treated in greater detail than any other, and it also includes recommendations on law, prisons, taxation, fortifications, coinage, manufacturing, trade, administrations, and spies (Violatti 2013).

> When Kautalya used the term as the title of his manual, it embraced a far wider field that included every aspect of economic, social and political life, including what we would call political economy and government policy. The lawgivers did not recommend an ascetic mode of life for everyone (Ambirajan 1997).

The Arthashastra broadly covers 14 areas:

I. Deals with the king—his training, appointments of ministers, and so on

II. Describes the duties of various officers of the state and gives a complete picture of the state's activities

III. Concerned with law and administration of justice

IV. Suppression of crimes

V. A sundry collection of topics including the salaries of officials

VI. Foreign policy and constituent elements of state

VII. An exhaustive discussion of the way in which each of the six methods of foreign policy may be used in various situations

VIII. Relates to calamities

IX. Preparations of war

X. Concerned with fighting and types of battle arrays

XI. How must a conqueror deal with a number of chiefs rather than one king

XII. Shows how a weak king when threatened by a stronger one must overpower him

XIII. Concerned with the conquest of the enemy's fort by fighting

XIV. Deals with occult practices

The *Arthashastra* provides information "not only to understand government and administration about the beginning of the 3rd century BC but also information on Indian medicine, mining, census taking, meteorology, shipping, surveying, and so on, and above all to observe many aspects of Indian life" (Thanawala 1997).

To appreciate the *Arthashastra*, it may be helpful to know something about its author and the regime in which he lived. Kautilya, also known as Chanakya and as Vishnugupta, was an adviser to King Chandragupta, who ruled in Northern India circa 322 to 298 BC. He has been credited as being the person who helped Chandragupta Maurya in overthrowing the Nanda dynasty and who installed him as the king of Magadha in Northern India. He is recognized as one of the earliest Indian philosophers to write about economics and politics. "All authorities agree that it was mainly because of *Kautilya* that the Mauryan Empire under *Chandragupta* and later under Asoka (reigned circa 265 to 238 BC) became a model of efficient government" (Encyclopedia Britannica 1974).

The ideas expressed by Kautilya in the *Arthashastra* are completely practical and unsentimental. Kautilya openly writes about controversial topics such as assassinations, when to kill family members, how to manage secret agents, when it is useful to violate treaties, and when to spy on ministers. Because of this, Kautilya is often compared to the Italian Renaissance writer Niccolò di Bernardo dei Machiavelli (1469 to 1527), author of *The Prince*, who is considered by many as unscrupulous and immoral. It is fair to mention that Kautilya's writing is not consistently without principles in that he also writes about the moral duty of the king. He summarizes the duty of a ruler, saying, "The happiness of the subjects is the happiness of the king; their welfare is his. His own pleasure is not his good but the pleasure of his subjects is his good." Some scholars have seen in the ideas of Kautilya a combination of Chinese Confucianism and Legalism (Violatti 2013). Let us analyze some of the salient features of the *Arthashastra*.

The economy: The economy as described in the Arthashastra is completely dominated by the state. Private economic activity other than crop production was only residual and even then subject to strict government regulation and control (Thanawala 1997). There is an implicit assumption that individual behavior could be controlled to a significant degree through economic rewards and penalties. Kautilya looked at economic issues from the perspective of an administrator. But he recognized that regulations must be consistent with human propensities in the economic sphere. He also seemed to be aware that controls must encourage rather than repress desirable economic activity. It is important to note that the primary purpose of Kautilya's *Arthashastra* was instruction of the king in the business of extending and preserving his dominion, by whatever means, political, economic, that seem suitable to his end.

Agriculture: Kautilya emphasized the predominance of agriculture and animal husbandry. Vakil (1970) has emphasized that cattle breeding was regarded as the basic source of new wealth. Agriculture was the highest occupation in the society—a society that was characterized by occupational division. Agricultural techniques were well developed and methods of improving the cultivation of land were known and implemented. Land revenue was the largest source of state income, and land values were assessed with fertility as the major consideration. In order to save the cultivators from the clutches of traders, the state fixed prices on all agricultural produce. Land was considered to be the source of all wealth. Labor and capital are also mentioned as instruments for the creation of wealth.

Private property: Kautilya supported the institution of private property. But the right of property was restrained in various ways. Group organization was accepted as the normal form of economic life. Thus, the determining factors were both custom and contract. The early Indian scriptures described material or worldly success not only as morally desirable but also as an essential stage in a full and civilized life. The rational and systematic pursuit of gain (including material gain) was, at the very least, not inconsistent with a moral life as long as such a pursuit did not violate basic moral norms (Vakil 1970).

Income inequalities: Startling inequalities in income were not very common. According to Aiyangar (1934) the laws of inheritance, taxation, and rules determining the conditions of work and expenditure were so devised that it was difficult for big fortunes to arise. Besides, wealth was not considered a social ladder for advancement. And caste stratification did not coincide with economic stratification. Income distribution was based on the principle of services rendered and on the personal and human needs of every individual. Income derived by owners of land was treated as rent. The right to rent was based on the scarcity of arable land and its productivity. The productiveness of land was dependent on its fertility, both natural and acquired, and its accessibility as determined by its proximity to a market and the cost of transport.

Kautilya's labor theory of value: Two millennia before Adam Smith enunciated the labor theory of value, Kautilya in the *Arthashastra* held that a "just" wage to be paid to workers should be based on the amount of time spent on the job, the amount of output created, and the skills necessary to perform the required tasks. Kautilya explicitly recognizes three distinct components for determining the market value of labor: the level of skill required (the human capital element), labor hours worked, and units of output produced (the labor productivity element). As stated by Sen (1967)

> a uniform and flat rate of wages for laborers of all sorts is impracticable in an advanced economic condition where commodities of various gradations of value representing different kinds and degrees of manufacturing skill are produced and used by consumers. The wages of a laborer cannot but be dependent on the market-value of the article produced. The latter again depends on the cost of its production, including the cost of material used. Thus the settlement of just wages is a complicated matter depending not only on the skill of the worker employed but also on the total out-turn of his work; i.e., both the quality and quantity of the job completed by him.

R. Shamasastry in his translation, *Kautilya's Arthashastra*, cites that among the duties of the superintendent of weaving shall be the setting of wages paid to weavers. Wages shall be fixed on the basis of whether the threads spun are fine, coarse, or of middle quality; in proportion to a greater or lesser quantity manufactured; and in consideration of the quantity of thread spun. Wages shall be cut short, if, making allowance of the quality of raw material, the quantity of the thread spun out is found to fall short. In determining wages for labor in general, Sen (1967) has referred to the quotes of Shamasastry in establishing the following procedure. "As to wages not previously settled, the amount shall be fixed in proportion to the work done and the time spent in doing it. Wages being previously unsettled, a cultivator shall obtain one-tenth of the crops grown, a herdsman one-tenth of the butter clarified, a trader one-tenth of the sale proceeds. Wages previously settled shall be paid and received as agreed upon." To prevent deception by employers, Kautilya lays down that cultivators or merchants shall either at the end or in the middle of their cultivation or manufacture pay the laborers proportionate wages. Payment to labor is not contingent on the marketing of goods. Production should not be hampered by the irresponsible conduct of the workers (Sen 1967). Guilds of Artisans (*Sanghabhrta*) often functioned as contractors and employed semiskilled and unskilled laborers. To protect these laborers, Kautilya recommends that a board of overseers review the guild contracts concerning wage rates and working conditions.

Kautilya was far ahead of his time in developing a labor theory of value in trying to determine what was a "just" wage for workers. Anticipating the thoughts of Smith and Ricardo, he explicitly recognized that the value of labor depends on the level of skills employed, time spent on the job, and the amount of output produced. He was also cognizant that the market value of labor reflects the market value of the product created. One can only conjecture that trade theory, principles of taxation, and the labor theory of value associated with classical economic thought might have evolved much earlier (perhaps in the 14th or 15th centuries) if Kautilya's views had been known to scholars such as St. Thomas Acquinas in the late middle ages or early Mercantilists in the Renaissance. This is another example of occidental philosophical thought suffering from not having access to oriental philosophical thought (Waldauer, Zahka, and Pal 1996).

International trade: The importance of international trade is emphasized by Kautilya in that he advises the sovereign that foreign relations should be guided strongly by trade considerations. His views on international trade are most clearly spelled out in Book II of the *Arthashastra*; Chapter XVI specifies the duties of the king's superintendent of commerce. He counsels that relationships with southern kingdoms are to be favored over those with northern kingdoms because the southern kingdoms possess greater mineral wealth (Sen 1967). Kautilya also saw advantages in attracting foreigners who possessed good technical and other economic development insights of the realm.

> Unlike the Mercantilists, *Kautilya* also explicitly recognizes that imports represent a very important way in which the wealth of the realm can be increased, in that imports can provide the kingdom with products which are either not available domestically (e.g., natural resources and agricultural commodities) or can be obtained more cheaply from foreign sources through trade than through domestic production. Kautilya fully realizes that exports

are not more important than imports as a means for enhancing the kingdom's wealth. He explicitly formulates a comparative advantage view of international trade patterns by stating that it is mutually beneficial to the various kingdoms when the products being imported are cheaper than those that can be obtained domestically and will fetch higher prices to the exporter than can be gotten in domestic markets. (Sen 1967)

Kautilya proposes heavy state regulation of trade, both so as not to undermine state monopolies and not to aid potential adversarial kingdoms. He also advocates price and profit controls, being concerned about "just" and "fair" prices and profits. Kautilya imposed a heavy taxation on imported foreign goods of luxury. On the articles of common consumption, light duties were imposed (Choudhary 1971). Kautilya supports the use of tariffs, both import and export duties, primarily as revenue-raising devices for the monarch rather than as mechanisms for altering trade patterns. "Import rates, intended for revenues rather than for trade limitation, generally ranked between 4 per cent and 20 per cent ad valorem" (Braibanti and Spengler 1963). Kautilya urges the monarch to create trade missions to promote trade with other kingdoms and especially supports bilateral trade arrangements in products.

Public finance/taxation: Kautilya's principles of taxation were remarkable for how extensive they were and how well they conform to modern principles of good tax systems. Gopal (1940) has observed that "while taxation is necessary, Kautilya was aware of the limits to taxation. Taxes were regarded as payment due to the king." They were divinely ordained and also considered as "the wage of the King, his reward for protecting his subjects, his remuneration for being the servant of the people and his salary as a public functionary. There was an element of compulsion." In advising the ideal tax system, Kautilya enunciates a set of "principles of taxation" remarkably similar to the modern-day criteria first formulated by Adam Smith (1776) as "canons of taxation" in his *Wealth of Nations*. Kautilya recognizes that the "ideal" tax system should embody the principles of convenience to pay, easy to calculate, inexpensive to administer, fair (equitable) in its burden, nondistortive of economic behavior in its impact (neutral), and in general not inhibit economic growth and development" (Gopal 1940).

Thus, Kautilya's views on the elements of a good tax system predate modern economic thought by some 2,000 years: "Kautilya's discussion of taxation and expenditure, apparently in keeping with traditional doctrine, gave expression to three Indian principles: taxing power is limited; taxation should not be felt to be heavy or exclusive; tax increases should be graduated" (Spengler 1971). Kautilya recognized that a prosperous and stable kingdom had to be founded on a well-developed and well-administered tax system. The importance of public finance to the successful reign by a monarch is underscored by his succinct advice to his sovereign. Since all activities depend on finance, financial troubles are more serious (Gopal 1940). In Kautilya's view, finance was so important to the success and well-being of the sovereign that it, along with the army, was under the direct control of the king. Kautilya advocates a highly structured and centralized revenue system, with extensive use of broad-based taxes. The system is supervised by the collector-general of revenues (*Samaharta*), who reports directly to the monarch and is equal in importance and influence to the commander-in-chief of the army. All the superintendents of the king whose activities generate revenues for the sovereign report to the collector-general of revenues.

Kautilya advises that taxation should not be raised to such a high degree that it destroys people's economic incentives to engage in productive undertakings, thereby lowering the level of economic activity and the material wealth of the kingdom (Gopal 1940). The amount of tax liability should be certain and known, and convenient to pay. Thus, Kautilya clearly enunciated well before the rise of classical economic thought a detailed, all-inclusive, and effective tax system. The principle of progression was followed and double taxation was regarded as unfair.

Salaries of (state) servants: "Kautilya was very much concerned about judicious use of the tax revenue. Exactly on the lines of the modern 'pay commissions' that get constituted by governments for fixing wages, salaries, and revenue expenditures of the government, Kautilya had prepared a thorough list for annual wages and salaries to be paid to the government employees as also for other revenue expenditures. While his attention to such minute details of administrative payments was noteworthy, what was even more remarkable was his mindfulness of the need to preserve substantive revenue for public goods. He categorically mentioned that wages and salaries of the state should not exceed 25 per cent of the total revenue. Once again, this is reminiscent of present day governments being advised by economic advisers to shun revenue deficits. Saletore (1963) had summed up well when he said that Kautilya's theory of public finance was both comprehensive and probably the World's most ancient" (Deodhar 2018, pp. 19–20).

To conclude, Kautilya was a pioneer in diplomacy and government administration. His merit was based not only on coming up with very important practical advice for government, but also in organizing his theories in a systematic and logical fashion. Kautilya's political vision had a heavy influence on Chandragupta, the first Indian ruler who unified Northern India under a single political unit. Even today, the *Arthashastra* is the number one classic work on diplomacy in India, and within this category, it is one of the most complete works of antiquity. A number of institutions in India, such as universities and diplomatic offices, have been named after Kautilya in honor of his work. Even important political figures of contemporary India, have been influenced by Kautilya's ideas (Violatti 2013). The *Arthashastra* deals with a self-sufficient economy based on indigenous ways of production as well as distribution and trade, and discusses monetary and fiscal policies, welfare, international relations, and war strategies in detail. It depicts in many ways the India of Kautilya's dreams.

The economics part of Kautilya's *Arthashastra* is nothing but a manual of public finance with detailed descriptions of economic offences and punishments. It can be confidently stated that economic ideas in India—just as in classical Greece—dealt with the improvement of human behavior through teachings and legal regulations that would contribute to the emergence of an orderly and stable economic organization. The stress was not on the growth of the economies as such, but rather conservation, sharing, and the prevention of injustice through escape from the rigors of scarcity caused by inhospitable geographical conditions, unexpected disasters, and above all by a fickle and basically greedy human nature (Ambirajan 1997).

Table 13.1 Concepts developed and used by Kautilya

Re-emerged during the period	Concepts Originated and applied by Kautilya
1700–1850	Gains from trade, diversification, division of labor, inter-temporal choice, labor theory of property, law of diminishing returns, moral hazard, regulation of monopoly, sources of economic growth, Dupuit Curve, principles of taxation
1850–1900	Distinction short run and long run, Efficiency Wages, externality, Demand-Supply Apparatus, Opportunity cost, Producer Surplus
1900–1970	Principal–agent problem, Liquidity, Mean-Variance approach, non-cooperative game
1970–Present	Asymmetric information, piece-wise linear income tax, loss-aversion, information economics, self-protection, self-insurance, time inconsistency, systemic risk

Source: Sihag (2014).

Sihag (2014) has contributed a very commendable book on Kautilya, and he has very cogently provided therein a list of concepts innovated and used by Kautilya along with their emergence in different time periods.

Sihag (2014) has characterized Kautilya as a one-man Planning Commission and more. Kautilya's *Arthashastra* is comprehensive, coherent, concise, and consistent. It consists of three fully developed but interdependent parts.

A) Principles and policies related to economic growth; taxation; international trade; efficient, clean, and caring governance; moral and material incentives to elicit effort; and preventive and remedial measures to deal with famines

B) Administration of justice, minimization of legal errors, formulation of ethical and efficient laws, labor theory of property, regulation of monopolies and monopsonies, protection of privacy, laws against sexual harassment and child labor

C) All aspects of national security: energetic, enthusiastic, well-trained, and well-equipped soldiers; most qualified and loyal advisers; strong public support; setting up an intelligence and analysis wing; negotiating a favorable treaty; military tactics and strategy; and diet of soldiers to enhance their endurance

Unlike his contemporary, Aristotle, Kautilya's views were unknown to medieval and Renaissance philosophers, and consequently, had no influence on the creation of modern economic theory. David Hume, Adam Smith, David Ricardo, and John Stuart Mill, among others, therefore, did not have the benefit of Kautilya's thoughts on the best policies and practices for creating and enhancing a nation's wealth (Waldauer, Zahka, and Pal 1996).

Endnote

1. Brainkart.com. n.d. "Contributions of Indian Economic Thinkers." https://www.brainkart.com/article/Contributions-of-Indian-Economic-Thinkers_33391/, (accessed August 10, 2019).

References

Acemoglu, D., S. Naidu, P. Restrepo, and J.A. Robinson. March, 2014. "Democracy Does Cause Growth." National Bureau of Economic Research, Working Paper 20004. https://www.nber.org/papers/w20004.pdf, (accessed April 22, 2019)

Agarwal, N. March 30, 2016. "India before 1991: Stories of Life under the License Raj." https://spontaneousorder.in/india-before-91/, (accessed April 27, 2019).

Ahmed, S., and A. Varshney. 2009. "Battles Half Won: The Political Economy of India's Growth and Economic Policy Since Independence," Commission on Growth and Development, Working Paper No. 15. http://citeseerx.ist .psu.edu/viewdoc/download?doi=10.1.1.207.2478&rep=rep1&type=pdf, (accessed May 17, 2019).

Aiyangar, R.K.V. 1934. *Aspects of Ancient Indian Economic Thought*. Benaras, India: Benaras Hindu University.

Aiyar, Y. and T.R. Raghunandan. February 25, 2015. "Whither decentralization?," *MINT* https://www.livemint.com/Opinion/ZBFTYAfcLkzBeyvsK33YAJ/ Whither-decentralization.html, (accessed on February 6, 2020).

Alagh, Y.K. June 30, 2018. "The Next Stage of Planning in India." *Economic and Political Weekly* III, Nos. 26 and 27. https://www.epw.in/system/files/ pdf/2018_53/26-27/CM_LIII_26%2627_300618_Yoginder_K_Alagh.pdf, (accessed April 17, 2019).

Alagh, Y.K. November 19, 2014. "Land, Air and Water: 2020 Is Not Far, Decide and Act Now," *Hindustan Times*. www.pressreader.com/india/hindustan-times-jalandhar/20141119/281840051969582, (accessed on April 17, 2019).

Alexander, S. July 2, 2019. "Fresh Investments Plunge to a 15-year low," *MINT*. https://www.livemint.com/news/india/new-investment-plunges-to-a-15-year-low-1561976363936.html, (accessed July 24, 2019)

Ali, M.A., 2003. "The Mughal Empire and Its Successors." https://en.unesco. org/silkroad/sites/silkroad/files/knowledge-bank-article/vol_V%20silk%20 road_the%20mughal%20empire%20and%20its%20sucessors.pdf.

Ambirajan, S. 1997. "The Concepts of Happiness Ethics, and Economic Values in Ancient Economic Thought." In *Ancient Economic Thought*, ed. B.B. Price. London, UK: Routledge Publication.

Arrow, K.J. 1951. *Social Choice and Individual Values.* New York, NY: John Wiley and Sons, Inc New York.

Asher, M.G. April 2, 1994. "Some Aspects of Role of the State in Singapore." *Economic and Political Weekly* 29, No. 14. https://www.epw.in/system/files/pdf/1994_29/14/special_articles_some_aspects_of_role_of_state_in_singapore.pdf, (accessed July 24, 2019).

Balakrishna, R. 1954. *Studies in Indian Economic Problems: Selected Essays.* Bangalore, India: The Bangalore Press.

Banerjee, N. January 8, 2015. "Will Niti Do Justice to Development?" *The Free Press Journal.* https://www.freepressjournal.in/editorspick/will-niti-do-justice-to-development/514245, (accessed April 17, 2019).

Bardhan, P. May, 2010. "Democracy and Development in India: A Comparative Perspective," Keynote lecture given at Sixty Years of Indian Democracy, Conference at Brown University, University of California, Berkeley, CA. http://eml.berkeley.edu/~webfac/bardhan/papers/DemDevIndia.pdf, (accessed April 20, 2019).

Basu, K. October, 2018. "A Short History of India's Economy: A Chapter in the Asian drama," United Nations University, WIDER Working Paper 2018/124. https://www.wider.unu.edu/sites/default/files/Publications/Working-paper/PDF/wp2018-124.pdf, (accessed April 19, 2019).

Basu, K., July 23, 2019. "Economic Graffiti: What is to be done about growth," National Council of Applied Economic Research (NCAER), New Delhi. http://www.ncaer.org/news_details.php?nID=292 (accessed on January 1, 2020).

Basu, P.K. 2008. "Reinventing Public Enterprises and Their Management as the Engine of Development and Growth." In *Public Enterprises: Unresolved Challenges and New Opportunities*, United Nation, New York, USA. https://publicadministration.un.org/publications/content/PDFs/E-Library%20Archives/2005%20EGM%20Public%20Enterprises_Unresolved%20Challenges%20and%20New%20Opportunities.pdf (accessed December 30, 2019).

Braibanti, R., and J.J. Spengler, eds. 1963. *Administration and Economic Development in India.* Durham, NC: Duke University Press.

Bremmer, I. June 29, 2019. "The Promise of Liberal Democracy Lives on within different Political Cultures," *Hindustan Times.* https://www.hindustantimes.com/columns/the-promise-of-liberal-democracy-lives-on-within-different-political-cultures/story-tprbl6v9BbVxKZvDlNf9VM.html, (accessed June 30, 2019).

Bueno de Mesquita, B., and G.W. Downs. September/October, 2005. "Development and Democracy: Richer but not Freer, Council on Foreign Relations. http://www.foreignaffairs.com/articles/61023/bruce-bueno-de-mesquita-and-george-w-downs/development-and-democracy, (accessed April 23, 2019).

Cairncros, A. 1966. *Introduction to Economics.* 4th ed. London, UK: Butterworth & Co. (Publishers) Ltd.

Chandar, Y.U. 2016. *The Ailing India*. Chennai, India: Notion Press.

Choudhary, R. 1971. *Kautilya's Political Ideas and Institutions*. Varanasi, India: Chowkhambra Sanskrit Studies Office.

Coase, R.H. October 1960. "The Problem of Social Cost." *Journal of Law and Economics* 3, The University of Chicago Press. https://www2.econ.iastate .edu/classes/tsc220/hallam/Coase.pdf, (accessed March 5, 2020).

Columbia University. n.d. "Economic and Social Developments under the Mughals." http://www.columbia.edu/itc/mealac/pritchett/00islamlinks/ikram/ part2_17.html, (accessed April 17, 2019).

Dab, J.K. June 18, 2016. "From Planning Commission to NITI Aayog: End of Nehruvian Legacy Challenges Ahead," *Mainstream Weekly.* http://www .mainstreamweekly.net/article6484.html, (accessed April 17, 2019).

Deaton, A. and J. Dreze. 2007. "Poverty and Inequality in India." In *Globalization and Politics in India*, ed. B.R. Nayar. New Delhi, India: Oxford University Press.

DeFrain, J. and S. Asay. 2012. *Strong Families Around the World: Strengths-Based Research and Perspectives*. New York, NY: Routledge, Taylor and Francis Group.

Deodhar, S.Y. January, 2018. "Indian Antecedents to Modern Economic Thought," IIMA, W. P. No. 2018-01-02. https://seminar.iima.ac.in/assets/snippets/work-ingpaperpdf/3431835162018-01-02.pdf, (accessed August 14, 2019).

Desai, M. August 15, 2016. "The Unfinished Agenda of Reform," *The Financial Express.* https://www.financialexpress.com/opinion/the-unfinished-agenda-of-reform/347614/, (accessed July 22, 2019).

Desai, M. April 21, 2019a. "Out of My Mind: New Hegemonic Order Set to Take Over," *The Indian Express.* https://indianexpress.com/article/opinion/ columns/out-of-my-mind-new-hegemonic-order-set-to-take-over-elections-india-democracy-5686248/, (accessed April 20, 2019).

Desai, M. June 30, 2019b. "Out of My Mind: It Is Democracy That Unites India," *The Indian Express.* https://indianexpress.com/article/opinion/col-umns/out-of-my-mind-new-hegemonic-order-set-to-take-over-elections-india-democracy-5686248/, (accessed July 14, 2019).

Dixit, A. K. 2004. Lawlessness and Economics: Alternative Modes of Governance, Princeton University Press, Princeton, New Jersey, USA

Dutt, R.C. 1963. *The Economic History of India 1757-1837*. New Delhi, India: Government of India.

Elphinstone, M. 2013. *The History of India: Volume 2, Cambridge Library Collection—Perspectives from the Royal Asiatic Society*. New Delhi, India: Cambridge University Press.

Ellis, C. 2017. *Colonial and Postcolonial South Asia*. New York, NY: Britannica Educational Publishing in association with The Rosen Publishing Group, Inc.

Encyclopedia Britannica. n.d.a. "Agriculture, Forestry, and Fishing." https:// www.britannica.com/place/India/Agriculture-forestry-and-fishing, (accessed July 29, 2019).

Encyclopedia Britannica. n.d.b. "Demographic Trends." https://www.britannica.com/place/India/Demographic-trends

Encyclopedia Britannica. n.d.c. "History." https://www.britannica.com/place/India/History.

Encyclopedia Britannica. n.d.d. "Politics and the Economy." https://www.britannica.com/place/India/Politics-and-the-economy#ref47004.

Encyclopedia Britannica. n.d.e. "The Mutiny and Great Revolt of 1857–59." https://www.britannica.com/place/India/The-mutiny-and-great-revolt-of-1857-59.

Encyclopedia Britannica. n.d.f. "The Transfer of Power and the Birth of Two Countries." https://www.britannica.com/place/India/The-transfer-of-power-and-the-birth-of-two-countries.

Ersson, S., and J.-E. Lane. 1996. "Democracy and Development: A Statistical Exploration." In *Democracy and Development*, ed. A. Leftwich. Cambridge, UK: Polity Press.

Bernier, F. 1916. *Travels in the Mogul Empire, A.D. 1656-1668*. Mumbai, India: Oxford University Press.

Fukuyama, F. 2014. *Political Order and Political Decay: From the Industrial Revolution to the Globalization of Democracy*. New York, NY: Farrar, Straus and Giroux.

Fukuyama, F., 2019. "Against Identity Politics, The Andrea Mitchell Center for the Study of Democracy." https://www.sas.upenn.edu/andrea-mitchell-center/francis-fukuyama-against-identity-politics, (accessed July 17, 2019).

Gadgil, D.R. 1938. *The Industrial Evolution of India in Recent Times*. London, UK: Oxford University Press.

Ghate, C. and S. Wright. 2010. "India's Growth Turnaround," Indian Statistical Institute, Delhi Center, IGC-ISI Conference, December 20-21, New Delhi, India. https://www.isid.ac.in/~cghate/Concise_OUP_GWF.pdf, (accessed July 18, 2019).

Gopal, M.H. April, 1940. "The Return of Classicism and after." *Indian Journal of Economics* XX, University of Allahabad, India.

Gosai, Dushyant, April 24, 2013. History of Economic Growth in India. https://intpolicydigest.org/2013/04/24/history-of-economic-growth-in-india/ (accessed December 25, 2019).

Guhan, S. January 24, 1998. "World Bank on Governance A Critique." *Economic and Political Weekly* 33, No. 4. https://www.epw.in/system/files/pdf/1998_33/4/world_bank_on_governance.pdf, (accessed April 18, 2019).

Habib, I. 2013. *The Agrarian System of Mughal India: 1556-1707, Oxford India Perennials Series*. 3rd ed. New Delhi, India: Oxford University Press.

Heo, U., and A.C. Tan. July, 2001. "Democracy and Economic Growth: A Causal Analysis." Comparative Politics 33, No. 4. https://www.jstor.org/stable/422444?seq=1#page_scan_tab_contents, (accessed April 20, 2019).

Hosmani, R.D. June 2014. "Trade and Commerce in Mughal Period," *International Journal of Scientific Research (IJSR)*, 3(6), ISSN No. 2277–8179. https://www.worldwidejournals.com/international-journal-of-scientific-research-(IJSR)/fileview.php?val=June_2014_1401774411_da143_63.pdf (accessed December 23, 2019)

Hudson, D. 2015. *Global Finance and Development*. New York, NY: Rutledge.

Hussain, Z. June 1, 2014. "Can Political Stability Hurt Economic Growth?" https://blogs.worldbank.org/endpovertyinsouthasia/can-political-stability-hurt-economic-growth, (accessed April 20, 2019).

Inglehart, R., and C. Welzel. March/April, 2009. "How Development Leads to Democracy: What We Know About Modernization." https://www.foreignaffairs.com/articles/2009-03-01/how-development-leads-democracy, (accessed April 23, 2019).

Joshi, V. 2016. *India's Long Road: The Search for Prosperity*. Gurugram, India: Penguin Books Limited.

Joshi, V. February, 2018. "India's Economic Reforms: Reflections on the Unfinished Agenda," Fifteenth L. K Jha Memorial lecture delivered on December 11, 2017, *RBI Bulletin*. https://rbidocs.rbi.org.in/rdocs/Bulletin/PDFs/02S P10021840CF3ECE274447F1824D42D94C41A427.PDF, (accessed July 29, 2019).

Kadekodi, G.K., and S.V. Hanagodimath. May 2, 2015. "Does Development Motivate More to Vote?" *Economic and Political Weekly* 50, No. 18. https://www.epw.in/system/files/pdf/2015_50/18/SA_L_18_020515_Gopal_K_Kadekodi.pdf, (accessed April 22, 2019).

Kalbag, C. July 12, 2019. "Here's the Stuff of Legend," *The Economic Times*. https://www.pressreader.com/india/the-economic-times/20190712/282265256999849, (accessed July 24, 2019).

Kapur, M. June–September, 1997. *Fifty years of the Indian capital market: 1947-97*, Occasional Paper, RBI, Vol. 18(2–3).

Kelkar, V. January 28, 2019, "Pitches for NITI Aayog 2.0." http://shalksoftech.co.in/banking-finance-accounts/vijay-kelkar-ex-chairman-of-finance-commission-pitches-for-niti-aayog-2-0/, (accessed April 17, 2019).

Kotwal, A., B. Ramaswami, and W. Wadhwa. December, 2011. "Economic Liberalization and Indian Economic Growth: What's the Evidence?" *Journal of Economic Literature* 49, No.4. https://www.researchgate.net/publication/226652247_Economic_Liberalization_and_Indian_Economic_Growth_What's_the_Evidence, (accessed April 27, 2019).

Leonard, K. April 1979. "The 'Great Firm' Theory of the Decline of the Mughal." *Comparative Studies in Society and History*, 21, No. 2, Cambridge University Press.

Lewis, W.A. 1955. *Theory of Economic Growth*. London, UK: George Allen & Unwin Ltd.

Liberhan, R. August 24, 2015. "Democracy and Economic Growth—Partners or Opponents," *Financial Express*. https://www.financialexpress.com/opinion/democracy-and-economic-growth-partners-or-opponents/124456/, (accessed April 22, 2019).

Maddison, A. 2003. *The World Economy: Historical Statistics*. Paris, France: Organization for Economic Co-operation and Development (OECD).

Maddison, A. 2006. *Class Structure and Economic Growth: India & Pakistan since the Moghuls*. New York, NY: Routledge.

Maddison, A. 2007. *Contours of the World Economy 1-2030 AD: Essays in Macro-Economic History*. New Delhi, India: Oxford University Press.

Mahapatra, R. December 20, 2018. "Niti Aayog's New Strategy: A Call for Growth or Acceptance of Failure." https://www.downtoearth.org.in/blog/governance/niti-aayog-s-new-strategy-a-call-for-growth-or-acceptance-of-failure-62556, (accessed on April 17, 2019).

Mahalanobis, P.C. 1961. *Talks on Planning*. Calcutta, India: Asia Publishing House and Indian Statistical Institute.

_____ 1963. *The Approach to Operational Research to Planning in India*. Calcutta, India: Asia Publishing House and Indian Statistical Institute.

Maira, A. December 21, 2017. "India Cannot Take Shortcuts to Development," *MINT*. https://www.livemint.com/Opinion/YjRoL1vOqX0Gs4vUAR1hPJ/India-cannot-take-shortcuts-to-development.html, (accessed July 25, 2019).

Maira, A. February 17, 2010. "Indian Democracy & Development," *The Economic Times*. https://economictimes.indiatimes.com/indian-democracy-development/articleshow/5582289.cms, (accessed April 22, 2019).

Mehta, R. April 12, 1997. "Trade Policy Reforms, 1991-92 to 1995-96-Their Impact on External Trade." *Economic and Political Weekly* 32, No. 15. https://www.epw.in/system/files/pdf/1997_32/15/special_articles_trade_policy_reforms_1991_92_to_1995_96.pdf, (accessed April 28, 2019).

Misra, B.M. June -September, 1997. *Fifty years of the Indian capital market: 1947-97*, Occasional Paper, RBI, Vol. 18(2–3).

Mohan, R. 1992. "Industrial Policy and Controls." *In The Indian Economy: Problems and Prospects*, ed. B. Jalan. Viking, New Delhi: Penguin Books.

Mohapatra, S. K. June-September, 1997. *Poverty Alleviation: Anathema of the Indian Experience*, Occasional Paper, RBI, Vol. 18(2–3).

Morris, M.D. December, 1963. "Towards a Reinterpretation of Nineteenth-Century Indian Economic History." *Journal of Economic History* 23, p. 4.

Mukherjee, S. August 16, 2014. "Planning Decommissioned," *Business Standard*. https://www.business-standard.com/article/economy-policy/planning-decommissioned-114081600642_1.html, (accessed April 17, 2019).

Mukherji, R. February 19, 2009. "The State, Economic Growth, and Development in India." https://www.tandfonline.com/doi/full/10.1080/14736480802665238, (accessed April 27, 2019).

Mukhia, H. 2004. *The Mughals of India*. Oxford, UK: Blackwell Publishing Ltd.

Mundle, S. June 20, 2019. "How Will the Modi Government Leverage Its Massive Mandate?" *MINT.* https://www.livemint.com/opinion/online-views/opinion-how-will-the-modi-government-leverage-its-massive-mandate-1561054926980 .html, (accessed July 24, 2019).

Naoroji, D. 1902. *Poverty and Un-British Rule in India*. New Delhi, India: Publications Division, Ministry of Information and Broadcasting, Government of India; Commonwealth Publishers, 1988.

Nayyar, D. August 11, 2001. "Democracy and Development: The Indian Experience," Prem Bhatia Memorial lecture, India International Centre, New Delhi, India. http://prembhatiatrust.com/2001/08/11/lecture-6/, (accessed April 20, 2019).

Nayyar, D. 2006. "India's Unfinished Journey: Transforming Growth into Development." *Modern Asian Studies* 40, No. 3.

Nehru, J. 1946. *The Discovery of India*. New Delhi, India: Oxford University Press.

Oates, W. 1977. *The Political Economy of Fiscal Federalism*. Lexington, MA: Lexington Books.

Oommen, M.A. July 24, 2010. "Have the State Finance Commissions Fulfilled Their Constitutional Mandates?" *Economic and Political Weekly*, Vol. XLV No. 30. https://www.epw.in/system/files/pdf/2010_45/30/Have_the_State_Finance_Commissions_Fulfilled_Their_Constitutional_Mandates.pdf (accessed December 31, 2019).

Padmanabhan, A. August 15, 2016. "The Best Is Yet to Come for India," *MINT.* https://www.livemint.com/Opinion/eGPZMkqgr0pFczCPVCQKwL/The-best-is-yet-to-come-for-India.html, (accessed July 25, 2019).

Planning Commission, 1992 to 1997, 8th Five Year Plan (Vol-2), Government of India (GoI), New Delhi.

Pletcher, K. 2011. *The History of India*. New York, NY: Britannica Educational Publishing in association with Rosen Educational Services.

Pennar, K. June 7, 1993. "Is Democracy Bad for Growth?" *Bloomberg.* https://www.bloomberg.com/news/articles/1993-06-06/is-democracy-bad-for-growth, (accessed April 18, 2019).

Przeworski, A., and F. Limongi. 1993. "Political Regimes and Economic Growth." *Journal of Economic Perspectives* 7, No. 3. http://homepage.ntu.edu.tw/~kslin/macro2009/Przeworski&Limongi_1993.pdf, (accessed April 21, 2019).

Purushottam, S. June 1, 2019. "Why India Needs a Reindustrialisation Drive," *Financial Express.* https://www.financialexpress.com/opinion/why-india-needs-a-reindustrialisation-drive/1594907/, (accessed July 24, 2019).

Raghav, T. February 23, 2019. Explain economic inequality under Mughals. https://brainly.in/question/8364225. (accessed December 23, 2019).

Raj, P., and T. Sastry. April 18, 2019. "What do voters want? Better job opportunities tops the list." *The Hindu Business Line*. https://www.thehindubusinessline.com/opinion/what-do-voters-want-better-job-opportunities-tops-the-list/article26879080.ece (accessed January 1, 2020).

Rajagopalan, S. December 12, 2017. "State Capacity Freed Is State Capacity Built," *MINT*. https://www.livemint.com/Opinion/cVnodqEYEF2Uiua2nxQ2oN/State-capacity-freed-is-state-capacity-built.html, (accessed July 3, 2019).

Rajan, R. December 30, 2016. "Democracy, Inclusion and Prosperity," *MINT*. https://www.livemint.com/Opinion/rahmkurmguGzR334xGcuHK/Raghuram-Rajan--Democracy-inclusion-and-prosperity.html, (accessed April 23, 2019).

Ranade, M.G. 2018. "Essays On Indian Economics: A Collection of Essays and Speeches." London, UK: Forgotten Books.

Rangarajan, C. April 15, 2000. "State, Market and the Economy the Shifting Frontiers." *Economic and Political Weekly* 35, No. 16. https://www.epw.in/system/files/pdf/2000_35/16/State_Market_and_the_Economy.pdf, (accessed August 10, 2019).

Rangarajan, C. 2006. "Fiscal Federalism: Some Current Issues" *In India in a Globalising World: Some Aspects of Macroeconomy, Agriculture, and Poverty*, ed. Radhakrishna, et al. New Delhi, India: Academic Foundation.

Rangarajan, C. March 25, 2019. "Another Look at Fiscal Transfers," *The Hindu*. https://www.thehindu.com/opinion/lead/another-look-at-fiscal-transfers/article26626986.ece, (accessed July 15, 2019).

Rao, M.G. January 24, 2015a. "Role and Functions of NITI Aayog." *Economic and Political Weekly* 50, No. 4. https://www.epw.in/system/files/pdf/2015_50/4/Role_and_Functions_of_NITI_Aayog.pdf, (accessed April 17, 2019).

Rao, M. G., 2017. Central Transfers to States in India: Rewarding Performance While Ensuring Equity, NITI Aayog, New Delhi. https://www.niti.gov.in/niti/writereaddata/files/document_publication/Final%20Report_25Sept_2017.pdf (accessed December 31, 2019).

Rao, M.G. June 4, 2019. "Reformist government? Time for Modi sarkar 2.0 to walk the talk," *Financial Express*. https://www.financialexpress.com/opinion/reformist-government-time-for-modi-sarkar-2-0-to-walk-the-talk/1597122/ (accessed January 1, 2020).

Rao, S.L. May 13, 2015b. "Slow and Unsteady: Democracy Has Been a Hurdle to India's Development," *The Telegraph*. https://www.telegraphindia.com/opinion/slow-and-unsteady/cid/1440423, (accessed April 22, 2019).

RBI. March 31, 2003. "Report on Currency and Finance 2001-2002." https://rbidocs.rbi.org.in/rdocs/Publications/PDFs/35329.pdf, (accessed April 27, 2019).

Reddy, Y.V. January 31, 2017a. "India: In Search of Prosperity," *MINT*. https://www.livemint.com/Opinion/pfzw40UsAOgKyjkBs0xQeL/India-in-search-of-prosperity.html, (accessed July 29, 2019).

Reddy, Y.V. March 22, 2017b. State and the Market in India, Lecture delivered at Lecture Series of CVC, Central Vigilance Commission, New Delhi. http://www.yvreddy.com/state-market-india-22nd-march-2017/(accessed December 30, 2019)

Roy, T. 2002. "Economic History and Modern India: Redefining the Link." *Journal of Economic Perspectives* 16, No. 3. https://www.researchgate.net/publication/4746120_Economic_History_and_Modern_India_Redefining_the_Link, (accessed June 16, 2019).

Roy, T. 2016. "The British Empire and the Economic Development of India (1858-1947)," *Journal of Economic Literature* (JEL- Code-F54, N15, O10). https://pseudoerasmus.files.wordpress.com/2017/02/roy-2015-the-british-empire-and-the-economic-development-of-india-1858-1947.pdf (accessed December 24, 2019)

Sandesara, J.C. 1992. *Industrial Policy and Planning, 1947-91*. New Delhi, India: Sage Publication.

Sardana, M.M.K., December 7, 2010. "Democracy, Development and Growth: The Indian Experience," *ISID Discussion Notes*. http://isid.org.in/pdf/DN1004.pdf, (accessed July 17, 2019).

Sarkar, J.2009. *A Short History of Aurangzeb*. Hyderabad, India: Orient BlackSwan.

Schumpeter, J.A, 1954. *History of Economic Analysis*. London, UK: Allen & Unwin (Publishers) Ltd.

Sastri, K. A. N., and G. Srinivasachari 1982. *Advanced History of India*. New Delhi, India: Allied Publishers Pvt Ltd.

Sen, A. 1999. Democracy as a Universal Value, Journal of Democracy 10.3. https://www.unicef.org/socialpolicy/files/Democracy_as_a_Universal_Value.pdf (accessed December 31, 2019).

Sen, A. 2008. "Social Choice," *The New Palgrave Dictionary of Economics*, 2nd Ed., New York, NY: Springer.

Sen, B.C. 1967. *Economics in Kautilya*. Calcutta, India: Sanskrit College.

Sen, K. 2007. "Why Did the Elephant Start to Trot? India's Growth Acceleration Re-examined." http://citeseerx.ist.psu.edu/viewdoc/download?doi=10.1.1.5 09.3446&rep=rep1&type=pdf, (accessed June 16, 2019).

Sen, P. May 6, 2017. Plan, but Do Not Over-plan Lessons for NITI Aayog, Economic & Political Weekly, Vol. LII, No.18. https://www.epw.in/system/files/pdf/2017_52/18/SA_LII_18_060517_Pronab_Sen.pdf (accessed December 30, 2019)

Sharma, K.C. June–September, 1997. *Industrial Policy in India: Some Reflection*, Occasional Paper, RBI, Vol. 18(2–3).

Sharma, R.S. 2011. *Economic History of Early India*. New Delhi, India: Viva Books Pvt. Ltd.

Sihag, B.S. 2014. *Kautilya: The True Founder of Economics*. New Delhi, India: Vitasta Publications.

Sikuka, K. October 12, 2017. Is there a link between Democracy and Development in Africa? https://www.accord.org.za/conflict-trends/link-democracy-
development-africa/, (accessed on January 1, 2020).

Singh, N. July 16, 2019a. "A Question of Federalism," *Deccan Herald*. https://
www.deccanherald.com/opinion/main-article/a-question-of-federalism-
747361.html, (accessed July 17, 2019).

Singh, N, June 18, 2019b. "Economic challenges for the new government," *Financial
Express* https://www.financialexpress.com/opinion/economic-challenges-for-the-
new-government/1610571/, (accessed February 27, 2020).

Singh, S.K. 1999. "The State and the Market: The Indian Case." *In Liberalisa-
tion and Globalisation of Indian Economy*, Vol. 3 ed. K.R. Gupta. New Delhi,
India: Atlantic Publishers and Distributors.

Singh, S.K. 2009. "Some Aspects of Governance: An Analysis." In *Economics of
Good Governance*, ed. A.K. Thakur. New Delhi, Indian: Indian Economic
Association, Deep and Deep Publication.

Sirowy, L., and A. Inkeles. 1990. "The Effects of Democracy on Economic Growth
and Inequality: A Review." *Studies in Comparative International Development*
25, No. 1. https://link.springer.com/article/10.1007/BF02716908, (accessed
April 21, 2019).

Sivasubramonian, S. 2000. *The National Income of India during the Twentieth
Century*. New Delhi, India: Oxford University Press.

Smith, A. 1776. An Inquiry into the Nature and Causes of the Wealth of Nations, W. Strahan and T. Cadell, London.

Smith, N. August 17, 2016. "Economists Are Getting Real Jobs," *MINT*, https://
www.livemint.com/Opinion/LBqy1iF5ZMDiKUKrHWsiYK/Economists-
are-getting-real-jobs.html, (accessed July 22, 2019).

Spengler, J. 1980. *Origins of Economic Thought and Justice. Political & Social Economy*. Carbondale, IL: Southern Illinois University Press.

Spengler, J. 1971. *Indian Economic Thought*. Durham, NC: Duke University
Press.

Srinivasan, T.N., June, 1997. "Democracy, Markets, Governance and Development,"
Centre for Research on Economic Development and Policy Reform, Working Paper No. 7, Stanford, CA. https://kingcenter.stanford.edu/publications/
democracy-markets-governance-and-development, (accessed July 15, 2019).

Srivastava, D K, February 25, 2015. "Recommendations of the 14th Finance
Commission will change basic architecture of Centre-state fiscal ties," *The Economic Times*. https://economictimes.indiatimes.com/news/economy/policy/
recommendations-of-the-14th-finance-commission-will-change-basic-
architecture-of-centre-state-fiscal-ties/articleshow/46363348.cms?from=mdr
(accessed on February 6, 2020).

Szczepanski, K. July 8, 2019a. *The Mughal Empire in India.* https://www
.thoughtco.com/the-mughal-empire-in-india-195498 (accessed December
19, 2019).

Szczepanski, K. November 26, 2019b. *The British Rule in India: How British Rule
of India Came About —and How It Ended.* https://www.thoughtco.com/the-
british-raj-in-india-195275 (accessed December 19, 2019).

Tanzi, V. June 16, 2019. "Book Review—Challenges to Indian Fiscal Federalism by TM Thomas Issac, R Mohan and Lekha Chakraborty,"
Financial Express. https://www.financialexpress.com/lifestyle/book-review-
challenges-to-indian-fiscal-federalism-by-tm-thomas-issac-r-mohan-and-
lekha-chakraborty/1608854/, (accessed July 15, 2019).

Thanawala, K. 1997. "Kautilya's Arthashastra: A Neglected Work in the History of Economic Thought," In *Ancient Economic Thought*, ed. B.B. Price.
London, UK: Routledge Publication.

Thapar, R. 2002. *The Penguin History of Early India from the Origins.* New Delhi,
India: Penguin Books.

United Nations. 2008. "Public Enterprises: Unresolved Challenges and New
Opportunities," Publication based on the Expert Group Meeting on Re-
inventing Public Enterprise and their management, 27-28 October, 2005,
New York, United Nations, New York, NY, ST/ESA/PAD/SER.E/69.

Vakil, L.C. September, 1970. "Indian Economic Thought with Special Emphasis
on Gandhian Influence," A thesis submitted in partial fulfillment of the requirements for the degree Master of Arts, Department of Economics, Fresno
State College, Fresno, CA. file:///C:/Users/MAC/Downloads/VAKILle-
ana%20(2).pdf, (accessed September 12, 2019).

Vembu, V. April 10, 2019. "What These Elections Mean for the Economy,"
The Hindu Business Line. https://www.thehindubusinessline.com/opinion/
columns/the-cheat-sheet/what-these-elections-mean-for-the-economy/ar-
ticle26798187.ece, (accessed July 14, 2019).

Violatti, C. November 3, 2013. "Chanakya." https://www.ancient.eu/Kautilya/,
(accessed September 12, 2019).

Waldauer, C., W. Zahka, and S. Pal. 1996. "Kautilya's Arthashastra: A Neglected
Precursor to Classical Economics," *Indian Economic Review* 31, No. 1,
pp. 101-108. http://online.sfsu.edu/mbar/ECON605_files/Waldauer%20
et%20al%201996.pdf, (accessed September 14, 2019).

Washbrook, D.A. 2012. "The Indian Economy and the British Empire." In *India
and the British Empire*, eds. D. Peers, N. Gooptu. Oxford, UK: Oxford University Press.

About the Author

As an academician, **Shrawan Kumar Singh** has experience in teaching, research, and writing that spans over six decades. He has held academic positions at Indira Gandhi National Open University (IGNOU) (retired as professor and director of the School of Social Sciences); the University of Delhi (ARSD College); the Department of Economics, Faculty of Social Sciences, Banaras Hindu University (BHU); and Ranchi University (GLA College, Daltonganj). His field of interest covers Indian economic policy, business environment, and international business. He has a number of publications to his credit in the form of books, articles, and papers in various journals. He has been associated as visiting faculty with the Department of Commerce and Business Studies, University of Delhi; Sri Ram College of Commerce; Jamia Millia Islamia, Management Development Institute (MDI), Gurugram; and FORE School of Management, New Delhi.

He has participated in teleconferencing, audio–video programs, and phone-in-programs of Akashvani, Doordrashan, and other television channels. He has been a member of the University Grants Commission UGC Committee on Curriculum Development in Economics (2001), which recommended the UGC Model Curriculum in Economics for under- and postgraduate courses. He was a member of academic bodies of various Universities like the Academic Council and the Board of Courses of Studies as well as professional bodies. Recently, he contributed to UGC's e-PG *Pathshala* Project under the NMEICT mission of MHRD, Government of India, as a content writer in the field of business economics. His book *Understanding Demonetization in India: A Deft Stroke of Economic Policy* was published in April 2019 by Business Expert Press (BEP), New York, USA.

Index

OTHER TITLES FROM THE ECONOMICS AND PUBLIC POLICY COLLECTION

Jeffrey Edwards, North Carolina A&T State University, *Editor*

- *The Economics of Online Gaming: A Player's Introduction to Economic Thinking* by Andrew Wagner
- *Global Sustainable Capitalism* by Marcus Goncalves
- *Political Dimensions of the American Macroeconomy* by Gerald T. Fox
- *The Options Trading Primer: Using Rules-Based Option Trades to Earn a Steady Income* by Russell A. Stultz
- *A Guide to International Economics* by Shahruz Mohtadi
- *Foreign Direct Investment: The Indian Experience* by Leena Ajit Kaushal
- *Urban Development 2120* by Peter Nelson
- *Understanding Demonetization in India: A Deft Stroke of Economic Policy* by Shrawan Kumar Singh
- *Disaster Risk Management in Agriculture: Case Studies in South Asian Countries* by Huong Ha and R. Lalitha S. Fernando
- *The Option Strategy Desk Reference: An Essential Reference for Option Traders* by Russell A. Stultz
- *Disaster Risk Management: Case Studies in South Asian Countries* by Huong Ha and R. Lalitha S. Fernando
- *Economic Renaissance In the Age of Artificial Intelligence* by Apek Mulay
- *A Primer on Macroeconomics, Second Edition, Volume I: Elements and Principles* by Thomas M. Beveridge
- *A Primer on Macroeconomics, Second Edition, Volume II: Policies and Perspectives* by Thomas M. Beveridge
- *A Primer on Microeconomics, Second Edition, Volume I: Fundamentals of Exchange* by Thomas M. Beveridge
- *A Primer on Microeconomics, Second Edition, Volume II: Competition and Constraints* by Thomas M. Beveridge

Announcing the Business Expert Press Digital Library

Concise e-books business students need for classroom and research

This book can also be purchased in an e-book collection by your library as

- *a one-time purchase,*
- *that is owned forever,*
- *allows for simultaneous readers,*
- *has no restrictions on printing, and*
- *can be downloaded as PDFs from within the library community.*

Our digital library collections are a great solution to beat the rising cost of textbooks. E-books can be loaded into their course management systems or onto students' e-book readers.
The **Business Expert Press** digital libraries are very affordable, with no obligation to buy in future years. For more information, please visit **www.businessexpertpress.com/librarians**.
To set up a trial in the United States, please email **sales@businessexpertpress.com**.

www.ingramcontent.com/pod-product-compliance
Lightning Source LLC
Chambersburg PA
CBHW061217220326
41599CB00025B/4664